# Introduction

This workbook is cross-referenced to the revision guide, *AQA GCSE Additional Science Revision Plus*, published by Lonsdale.

The questions and activities are intended to reinforce your understanding of the three units of substantive content (Biology 2, Chemistry 2 and Physics 2), plus the procedural content (How Science Works), on the new single award GCSE Additional Science specification from AQA.

The questions in your exams will combine elements of both types of content, so to answer them you will have to recall relevant scientific facts and draw upon your knowledge of how science works. There are individual How Science Works worksheets throughout this book that are designed to help you practise these skills, for example, by evaluating social-scientific issues.

This workbook is suitable for use by Foundation and Higher Tier students.

**HT** Any material that is limited to Higher Tier students is clearly labelled and appears inside a grey tinted box.

## A Note to Teachers

The pages in this workbook can be used as…

- classwork sheets – students can use the revision guide to answer the questions
- harder classwork sheets – pupils study the topic and then answer the questions without using the revision guide
- easy-to-mark homework sheets – to test pupils' understanding and reinforce their learning
- the basis for learning homework tasks which are then tested in subsequent lessons
- test material for topics or entire units
- a structured revision programme prior to the objective tests / written exams.

Answers to these worksheets are available to order.

ISBN 978-1-905129-66

Published by Lonsdale, a division of Huveaux Plc

**Project Editor:** Rebecca Skinner

**Editors:** Charlotte Christensen and Tracey Cowell

**Cover and Concept Design:** Sarah Duxbury

**Design:** Graeme Brown and Little Red Dog Design

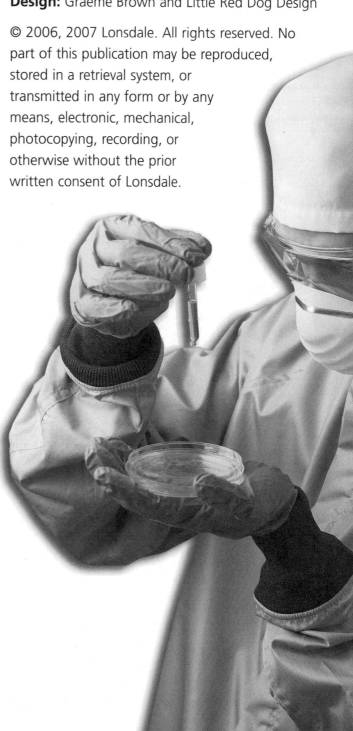

# Contents

# Contents

## Biology Unit 2

**4** What are animals and plants built from? (11.1)

**6** How do dissolved substances get into and out of cells? (11.2)

**7** How do plants obtain the food they need to live and grow? (11.3)

**10** What happens to energy and biomass at each stage in a food chain? (11.4)

**13** What happens to the waste material produced by plants and animals? (11.5)

**14** What are enzymes and what are some of their functions? (11.6)

**18** How do our bodies keep internal conditions constant? (11.7)

**22** Which human characteristics show a simple pattern of inheritance (11.8)

**31** Key Words

## Chemistry Unit 2

**32** How do sub-atomic particles help us to understand the structure of substances? (12.1) and How do structures influence the properties and uses of substances? (12.2)

**40** How much can we make and how much do we need to use? (12.3)

**49** How can we control the rates of chemical reactions? (12.4)

**53** Do chemical reactions always release energy? (12.5)

**60** How can we use ions in solutions? (12.6)

**69** Key Words

## Physics Unit 2

**70** How can we describe the way things move? (13.1)

**74** How do we make things speed up or slow down? (13.2)

**79** What happens to the movement energy when things speed up or slow down? (13.3)

**81** What is momentum? (13.4)

**85** What is static electricity, how can it be used and what is the connection between static electricity and electric currents? (13.5)

**89** What does the current through an electric circuit depend on? (13.6)

**93** What is mains electricity and how can it be used safely? (13.7)

**97** Why do we need to know the power of electrical appliances? (13.8)

**99** What happens to radioactive substances when they decay? (13.9)

**102** What are nuclear fission and nuclear fusion? (13.10)

**104** Key Words

There is a detailed periodic table on the inside back cover of this workbook for your reference.

The numbers in brackets correspond to the reference numbers on the AQA GCSE Additional Science specification.

# Biology Unit 2

## Typical Plant and Animal Cells

**1** Use the words below to label the two cell diagrams.

**Plant Cell**        **Animal Cell**        **Cell Wall**        **Chloroplasts**        **Ribosomes**

**Cell Membrane**        **Cytoplasm**        **Nucleus**        **Vacuole**

**2** Write the correct word alongside each definition.

**a)** The wall of a plant cell is made from this.

..............................................

**b)** Most cells have one of these; it contains genetic information.

..............................................

**c)** Chloroplasts contain this light-absorbing substance.

..............................................

**d)** All cells have one of these; it controls the movement of substances into and out of the cell.

..............................................

**3** Draw a line to connect each of the cells below to the correct description.

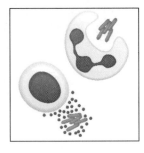 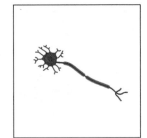  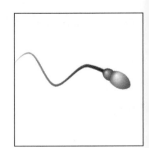

**Nerve cells** (neurones) have long slender structures which can carry nerve impulses over distances as long as one metre.

**The sperm cell** is the most mobile cell because of its tail. It has to travel from the vagina to the ovum.

**Red blood cells** have no nucleus so that they can be packed full of haemoglobin in order to carry lots of oxygen.

**White blood cells** can change their shape in order to engulf and destroy microbes which have invaded the body.

**To answer the questions on this page, you will have to recall scientific facts and draw upon your knowledge of how science works, e.g. scientific procedures, issues and ideas.**

**1** When an organism is in the first stages of development, all of its cells are the same. They then differentiate and become specialised. What is the reason for specialisation?

_____

**2** The organelle (parts of a cell) found in muscle cells include...

- cell membrane
- nucleus
- lots of mitochondria

- fibres that slide into each other, so the cell can change length
- cytoplasm (called sarcoplasm)

**a)** Which of these organelle can be found in other animal cells?

_____

**b)** Which of these organelle is unique to the muscle cell?

_____

**c)** Think about the role of muscles in the body. Why do you think it is important for muscle cells...

**i)** to be able to change length?

_____

_____

**ii)** to contain lots of mitochondria?

_____

_____

**3** Ciliated epithelial cells in the windpipe have tiny hair-like structures on the surface called cilia. When the cilia on lots of epithelial cells move together in a rhythmic motion, they can 'sweep' mucus away.

**a)** Ciliated epithelial cells always occur in large groups that form a tissue. Suggest one reason for this.

_____

**b)** Suggest one other place where you would expect to find ciliated epithelial cells.

_____

# Biology Unit 2

## Diffusion

**1** Why is it important for substances to be able to pass through the cell membrane to enter and leave a cell?

.................................................................................................................................................

.................................................................................................................................................

**2** Insert an arrow between the two boxes below, to indicate the direction in which particles move during diffusion.

| Low Concentration |     | High Concentration |
|---|---|---|

**3** Write **true** or **false**, as appropriate, alongside each of these statements about diffusion.

**a)** Diffusion is a passive process – it takes place automatically, without the need for energy. ...............

**b)** Diffusion can only take place through a cell membrane in one direction. ...............

**c)** Oxygen, glucose and ions all enter the cell from the blood by diffusion. ...............

**d)** Particles automatically move from a low concentration to a high concentration. ...............

**e)** Diffusion takes place where there is a concentration gradient, i.e. the concentration of particles inside the cell is different to the concentration of particles outside the cell. ...............

## Osmosis

**4** Insert an arrow between the two boxes below, to indicate the direction in which water molecules move during osmosis.

| Low Concentration |     | High Concentration |
|---|---|---|

**5** Sarah takes a beaker of water and adds some red food colouring. She then places a stalk of celery into the beaker and leaves it for 2 days. When Sarah returns, she finds that the leaves of the celery have turned red. Explain how this happened.

.................................................................................................................................................

.................................................................................................................................................

.................................................................................................................................................

## Making Food Using Energy from the Sun

**1** Write a dictionary-style definition for the word 'photosynthesis'. Remember, dictionary definitions use just a few well-chosen words to communicate an idea.

................................................................................................................................................................

................................................................................................................................................................

**2** What four things are needed for photosynthesis?

**a)** ....................................................................   **b)** ....................................................................

**c)** ....................................................................   **d)** ....................................................................

**3** Name each of the products of photosynthesis and for each one explain how the plant uses it.

**a)** ................................................................................................................................................................

................................................................................................................................................................

**b)** ................................................................................................................................................................

................................................................................................................................................................

**4** Complete the equation below to show the reaction that takes place during photosynthesis.

.......................... + .......................... $\longrightarrow$ .......................... + ..........................

**5** What substance, found in green plants, absorbs the light needed for photosynthesis?

................................................................................................................................................................

## Factors Affecting Photosynthesis

**6** The rate of photosynthesis in a plant slows down considerably in the evening. Suggest two possible reasons for why this happens.

**a)** ................................................................................................................................................................

................................................................................................................................................................

**b)** ................................................................................................................................................................

................................................................................................................................................................

# Biology Unit 2

## Factors Affecting Photosynthesis (cont.)

**7** A plant is placed in a sealed glass box. A constant temperature and light intensity are maintained and it is watered regularly.

**a)** Sketch a graph to show what you would expect to happen to the rate of photosynthesis over time.

**b)** Explain what is happening in your graph.

.......................................................................................................................................................

.......................................................................................................................................................

.......................................................................................................................................................

.......................................................................................................................................................

## Plant Mineral Requirements

**8** Plants need certain mineral ions for healthy growth.

**a)** Where do these mineral ions come from? .........................................................................................

**b)** How are these mineral ions taken in by the plant?

.......................................................................................................................................................

**c)** Why do plants need…

**i)** Nitrates? .............................................................................................................................

**ii)** Magnesium? ........................................................................................................................

**9** Jenna is growing some bamboo shoots in a glass of water on her window sill. They receive plenty of sunlight and are kept at a constant temperature, however, the leaves start to turn yellow. Suggest one possible reason for this.

.......................................................................................................................................................

**To answer the questions on this page, you will have to recall scientific facts and draw upon your knowledge of how science works, e.g. scientific procedures, issues and ideas.**

**1** A keen gardener is thinking about setting up a small business, selling home-grown strawberries. However, strawberries can be easily damaged by frost, so he decides to try growing some in a greenhouse.

He grows 100 plants in the greenhouse and 100 plants on the plot of land outside. The greenhouse uses natural light and air, but the temperature is kept at a constant 25°C.

The table above shows the fruit yield of the two groups of plants.

| Group (100 Strawberry Plants) | Fruit Yield (kg) |
| --- | --- |
| Plants Grown in Greenhouse | 43kg |
| Plants Grown Outdoors | 28kg |

**a)** Write a short conclusion based on these results.

............................................................................................................................................

............................................................................................................................................

............................................................................................................................................

**b)** To ensure a fair test, it is important to control the variables. Suggest two other factors that could have affected the results of this investigation.

**i)** ........................................................................................................................................

**ii)** .......................................................................................................................................

**c)** The optimum yield of strawberry plants is 0.5kg per plant.

**i)** What would be the optimum yield of 100 plants? ...............................................................

**ii)** Suggest one possible reason why the greenhouse plants in this investigation did not achieve this optimum yield.

............................................................................................................................................

**2** In terms of commercial fruit growing, name one other advantage of growing plants in a greenhouse.

............................................................................................................................................

**3** In terms of pest control, suggest one advantage of growing plants in a greenhouse.

............................................................................................................................................

# Biology Unit 2

## Food Chains

**1** Complete the flow chart using the words below, to show the order in which energy is transferred along a food chain.

| | | | |
|---|---|---|---|
| $\rightarrow$ | $\rightarrow$ | $\rightarrow$ | |

**Primary Consumer**          **Tertiary Consumer**          **Secondary Consumer**          **Producer**

**2** What is the original source of energy for all organisms? ........................................................

**3** Why are producers so important to a food chain?

.......................................................................................................................................................

**4** Producers all belong to the same group. Indicate which group, by putting a tick beside the correct option.

**a)** herbivores ☐          **b)** insects ☐          **c)** carnivores ☐          **d)** green plants ☐          **e)** omnivores ☐

**5** Describe how energy is lost at each stage of a food chain.

.......................................................................................................................................................

.......................................................................................................................................................

.......................................................................................................................................................

## Pyramids of Biomass

**6** What is meant by the term 'biomass'?

.......................................................................................................................................................

**7** Why does biomass decrease stage by stage as you move up a pyramid of biomass?

.......................................................................................................................................................

.......................................................................................................................................................

.......................................................................................................................................................

**8** Describe how the efficiency of food production in a food chain can be improved.

.......................................................................................................................................................

.......................................................................................................................................................

.......................................................................................................................................................

.......................................................................................................................................................

# How Science Works

To answer the questions on this page, you will have to recall scientific facts and draw upon your knowledge of how science works, e.g. scientific procedures, issues and ideas.

**1** Sketch a pyramid of biomass for each of the food chains shown below.

**a) Hosta (green plant)** ⟶ **Slug** ⟶ **Hedgehog** ⟶ **Badger**

**b) Green Algae** ⟶ **Tadpoles** ⟶ **Raft Spider** ⟶ **Fish** ⟶ **Otter**

# How Science Works

**To answer the questions on this page, you will have to recall scientific facts and draw upon your knowledge of how science works, e.g. scientific procedures, issues and ideas.**

**1** A farmer breeds cattle for beef. The animals are kept in enclosures inside a barn so that the temperature can be regulated and they cannot move around too much.

**a)** In terms of food production, explain why the farmer would want to…

   **i)** regulate the temperature of the environment in which the cattle are kept.

   ....................................................................................................................................................

   ....................................................................................................................................................

   **ii)** restrict how much the cattle can move around.

   ....................................................................................................................................................

   ....................................................................................................................................................

**b)** Suggest one other advantage of keeping the cattle inside a barn like this.

....................................................................................................................................................

**c)** Suggest one disadvantage for the farmer of raising cattle in this way.

....................................................................................................................................................

**d)** Some people object to livestock being raised in this way. Suggest one reason for this.

....................................................................................................................................................

**e)** There are strict guidelines and regulations in place to control the way in which farmers raise beef cattle. For example, it is prohibited to tie the animals up, because they need to be able to move freely and behave naturally.

Use the Internet (e.g. www.rspca.org.uk), school library or another secondary source to find one more example of a guideline relating to the care of beef cattle.  Explain the reason for the guideline.

Guideline: ......................................................................................................................................

....................................................................................................................................................

Reason: .........................................................................................................................................

....................................................................................................................................................

## Recycling the Materials of Life

**1** Producers take materials from the environment to help them live and grow. These materials are eventually returned to the environment. Name the two ways in which this happens.

**a)** ...................................................................................................................................................................

**b)** ...................................................................................................................................................................

**2 a)** In your own words, explain the role of microorganisms in this process.

**b)** Humans have learnt to use these microorganisms to help get rid of waste materials. Outline one example of this in practice.

## The Carbon Cycle

**3** Write the appropriate number alongside each explanation below, to show what stage of the carbon cycle it is describing.

**a)** Animals release $CO_2$ (a product of respiration) into the air. ☐

**b)** Microorganisms break down excrement and the bodies of dead animals and plants. ☐

**c)** Green plants take $CO_2$ from the atmosphere for photosynthesis. Some is returned during respiration. ☐

**d)** Microorganisms release $CO_2$ (a product of respiration) into the air. ☐

**e)** Carbon is converted into carbohydrates, fats and proteins by plants. When the plant is eaten, some of this carbon is then converted into carbohydrates, fats and proteins in the animal. ☐

☐

# Biology Unit 2

## Enzymes

**1 a)** Unscramble the letters to find three words that can be used to describe enzymes.

    **i) SCATTLAYS** ...........................................................................................................................................................

    **ii) TENIPOR** ...............................................................................................................................................................

    **iii) ADOMINICAS** ...................................................................................................................................................

**b)** Write a brief description of what an enzyme is, incorporating your three answers from part a).

.................................................................................................................................................................................................

.................................................................................................................................................................................................

.................................................................................................................................................................................................

**2** What is special about the shape of enzymes?

.................................................................................................................................................................................................

**3** What two factors can affect the action of enzymes?

**a)** ..................................................................................    **b)** ..................................................................................

**4 a)** What is the normal body temperature of a human being? .............................................................................

**b)** In terms of enzymes, explain why it is important for humans to maintain a fairly constant body temperature.

.................................................................................................................................................................................................

.................................................................................................................................................................................................

## Inside Living Cells

**5** Name two processes that occur in living cells and involve enzymes.

**a)** ..........................................................................................................................................................................................

**b)** ..........................................................................................................................................................................................

**6** Respiration in cells is the process by which glucose molecules are broken down to release energy. Describe one way in which this energy is used.

.................................................................................................................................................................................................

## Aerobic Respiration

**1** **a)** The parts of the body that enable breathing, e.g. the windpipe, lungs and diaphragm, are often referred to as the respiratory system. What is the difference between breathing and respiration?

......................................................................................................................................................

......................................................................................................................................................

**b)** Which gas must be present for aerobic respiration to be able to take place? ................................

**c)** Write a word equation for aerobic respiration.

......................................................................................................................................................

**d)** In what part of a living cell does aerobic respiration usually take place? ....................................

## Outside Living Cells

**2** What is the function of digestive enzymes?

......................................................................................................................................................

......................................................................................................................................................

**3** Complete the table below to show where the different digestive enzymes can be found, what substances they digest and what molecules are produced.

| Enzyme | Regions Where It is Found | What It Digests | Molecules Produced |
|--------|--------------------------|-----------------|--------------------|
| Protease | • <br> • <br> • | | Amino Acids |
| | • Pancreas <br> • Small Intestine | Lipids | |
| Amylase | • <br> • <br> • | Starch | |

**4** What are lipids? ...................................................................................................

# Biology Unit 2

## The Function of Bile

**1** Where is bile…

**a)** produced? _____   **b)** stored? _____

**c)** Summarise the two main functions of bile.

**i)** _____

_____

**ii)** _____

_____

**2** Many people suffer from gallstones. This can result in the removal of the gall bladder. State two possible problems this could cause.

**a)** _____

**b)** _____

## Use of Enzymes in the Home and Industry

**3** Washing detergents for clothes are described as biological or non-biological. Biological detergents contain enzymes. How does this help them to clean clothes more effectively?

_____

_____

**4** Explain how enzymes are used in the production of baby foods.

_____

_____

**5 a)** What function does isomerase perform?

_____

**b)** How do manufacturers take advantage of this in the production of slimming foods?

_____

# How Science Works

**To answer the questions on this page, you will have to recall scientific facts and draw upon your knowledge of how science works, e.g. scientific procedures, issues and ideas.**

**1** What is the function of enzymes?

.......................................................................................................................................................................................

**2 a)** How can enzymes help manufacturers save energy?

.......................................................................................................................................................................................

**b)** How does this benefit the environment?

.......................................................................................................................................................................................

**3** Describe two ways in which enzymes can be used in industry (other than those outlined on page 16).

**a)** ...............................................................................................................................................................................

.......................................................................................................................................................................................

**b)** ...............................................................................................................................................................................

.......................................................................................................................................................................................

**4** The manufacturers of biological washing powders recommend that you only use the powder for cool washes (up to 40°C).

**a)** Why is this?

.......................................................................................................................................................................................

**b)** Give one disadvantage of using enzymes in washing powders.

.......................................................................................................................................................................................

**5** Choose the correct words from the options below to complete this passage about one of the problems associated with using enzymes in industry.

Extracting enzymes is ................................, so it is important to be able to ................................ them as

often as possible. However, enzymes are ................................ in water, which makes it difficult to remove

them from ................................ after use if they are not ................................ first, i.e. trapped inside a

................................ material.

**re-use**     **liquids**     **immobilised**     **non-reactive**     **expensive**     **soluble**

# Biology Unit 2

## Controlling Conditions

**1** **a)** Which organ is responsible for monitoring and controlling blood glucose concentration? .............................

**b)** Which hormone does it produce to help maintain blood glucose levels? .............................

**c)** How does this hormone work?

.................................................................................................................................

.................................................................................................................................

.................................................................................................................................

## Blood Glucose Concentration

**2** Use the descriptions provided to complete the flow chart and show what happens when blood glucose concentration is too high.

| Blood Glucose Too High | → | Pancreas: | → | Liver: | → | Blood: |
|---|---|---|---|---|---|---|

| Glucose converted to glycogen | | Glucose removed | | Insulin released |
|---|---|---|---|---|

**3** **a)** What causes diabetes?

.................................................................................................................................

.................................................................................................................................

.................................................................................................................................

**b)** Name two ways in which blood glucose concentrations can be controlled in people with diabetes.

**i)** .............................................................................................................................

**ii)** .............................................................................................................................

## Body Temperature

**1** Body temperature is controlled by the nervous system.

**a)** Where are the receptors that provide information about blood temperature located? ...............................

**b)** Where are the receptors that provide information about skin temperature located? ...............................

**2** Explain why is it important to drink more water in hot weather.

.................................................................................................................................................................

.................................................................................................................................................................

**HT**

**3** Write **hot** or **cold** alongside each of these responses, to show the temperature conditions that trigger them.

**a)** Any sweating stops. ....................................

**b)** Blood vessels close to the skin's surface dilate. ....................................

**c)** Blood vessels close to the skin's surface constrict. ....................................

**4** In terms of heat loss, explain how the dilation or contraction of blood vessels close to the skin's surface helps to regulate temperature.

.......................................................................................................................................................

.......................................................................................................................................................

## Removing Waste Products

**5** Name two waste products that need to be removed from the body to maintain a constant internal environment. For each answer, state which process it is a product of and how it is removed.

**a)** Waste Product: ....................................................................................................................

A product of... ....................................................................................................................

Removed by... ....................................................................................................................

**b)** Waste Product: ....................................................................................................................

A product of... ....................................................................................................................

Removed by... ....................................................................................................................

# How Science Works

**To answer the questions on this page, you will have to recall scientific facts and draw upon your knowledge of how science works, e.g. scientific procedures, issues and ideas.**

**1** In the early 20th century, experiments carried out by Banting and Best led to the development of an effective treatment for diabetes.

**a)** How did Banting and Best establish that diabetes is linked to a problem with the pancreas?

_____

_____

**b)** In their subsequent experiments, what did the two scientists inject into diabetic dogs to try and control the disease?

_____

**c)** To produce a fair test, it is important to control the variables. Which variable did Banting and Best struggle to control?

_____

**d)** Banting and Best repeated their experiments many times with the same results. Why is it important to be able to do this?

_____

_____

**e)** Banting and Best carried out their research on dogs. In terms of understanding human diabetes, why might this have been a problem?

_____

**f)** Which hormone was discovered as a result of Banting and Best's experiments? _____

**g)** Before announcing their findings, Banting and Best only treated one human. Suggest a potential problem with this…

**i)** in terms of producing reliable evidence.

_____

**ii)** in terms of modern procedures for developing new drugs.

_____

# How Science Works

**To answer the questions on this page, you will have to recall scientific facts and draw upon your knowledge of how science works, e.g. scientific procedures, issues and ideas.**

**1** Insulin is used to help manage blood sugar levels in people with diabetes. It can be administered by injection or through an inhaler.

**a)** Which method has been around the longest? ................................................................................................

**b)** Is it an **advantage** or a **disadvantage** that this method has been around for a long time? Explain your answer.

........................................................................................................................................................................

........................................................................................................................................................................

........................................................................................................................................................................

**2** Describe two factors that can affect the absorption of injected insulin into the bloodstream.

**a)** ....................................................................................................................................................................

**b)** ....................................................................................................................................................................

**3** Why are insulin injections sometimes less effective in patients that smoke?

........................................................................................................................................................................

........................................................................................................................................................................

**4** Suggest two benefits of inhaling insulin.

**a)** ....................................................................................................................................................................

**b)** ....................................................................................................................................................................

**5** Why might insulin inhalers be more expensive than injections?

........................................................................................................................................................................

**6** Name one other potential problem with insulin inhalers.

........................................................................................................................................................................

**7** If insulin inhalers prove to be safe and effective, suggest one age group that might really benefit.

........................................................................................................................................................................

# Biology Unit 2

## Chromosomes

**1** For each question, indicate the correct answer by placing a tick in the box alongside it.

**a)** Human body cells contain a total of…

**i)** 23 chromosomes ☐

**ii)** 46 chromosomes ☐

**iii)** 22 chromosomes ☐

**b)** Sex cells are called…

**i)** genes ☐

**ii)** alleles ☐

**iii)** gametes ☐

**c)** Sex cells contain…

**i)** half the number of chromosomes of a body cell ☐

**ii)** the same number of chromosomes as a body cell ☐

**iii)** twice the number of chromosomes of a body cell ☐

## Inheritance of Sex – The Sex Chromosome

**2** Below are two sets of sex chromosomes. Write **male** or **female** alongside each one, to identify the sex of the individual they come from.

**a)** XY _____ **b)** XX _____

**3** Complete the genetic diagram below, to show all the possible permutations for sex inheritance.

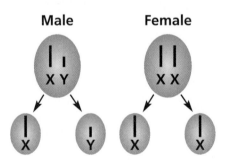

## Cell Division

**1** The following flow chart shows **mitosis**. Complete the chart by drawing a diagram for each stage.

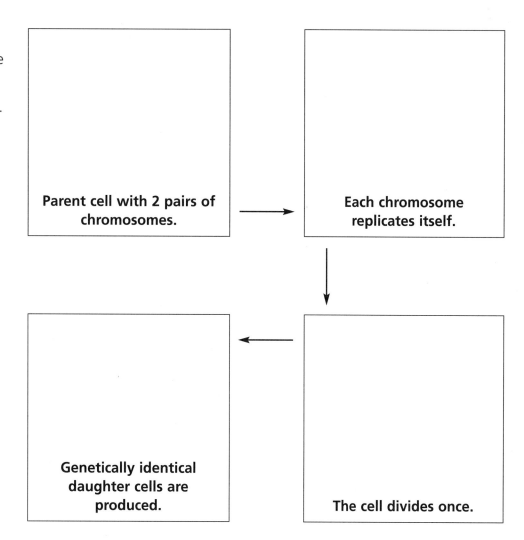

Parent cell with 2 pairs of chromosomes. → Each chromosome replicates itself.

Genetically identical daughter cells are produced. ← The cell divides once.

HT

**2** Use a line to connect the words 'meiosis' and 'mitosis' to the correct statements.

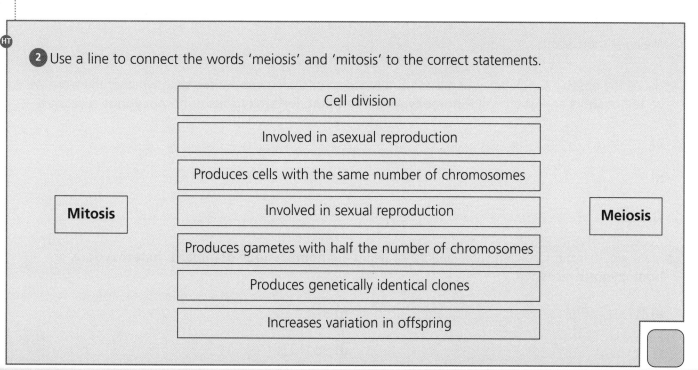

| Mitosis | Cell division | Meiosis |
| --- | --- | --- |
| | Involved in asexual reproduction | |
| | Produces cells with the same number of chromosomes | |
| | Involved in sexual reproduction | |
| | Produces gametes with half the number of chromosomes | |
| | Produces genetically identical clones | |
| | Increases variation in offspring | |

# Biology Unit 2

## Genetics

**1** Write dictionary-style definitions for the following words. Remember, dictionary definitions only use a few well-chosen words.

**a)** Allele ..................................................................................................................................................................

**b)** Dominant Allele ..................................................................................................................................................

.......................................................................................................................................................................................

**c)** Recessive Allele ..................................................................................................................................................

.......................................................................................................................................................................................

**2 a)** T is the allele for tongue rolling and t is the allele for non-tongue rolling. State whether the following individuals can roll their tongues or not.

**i)** tt ................................................................ **ii)** TT ................................................................

**iii)** tT ............................................................... **iv)** Tt ................................................................

**b)** B is the allele for brown eyes and b is the allele for blue eyes. State the colour of the following individuals' eyes.

**i)** Bb ............................................................... **ii)** bB ................................................................

**iii)** bb ............................................................... **iv)** BB ................................................................

**3** Scientists discovered a new species of plant, which occurs naturally in two different sizes. The height of the plant is determined by a single gene, which has two alleles. H is the dominant allele for tall plants, h is the allele for short plants.

List all the possible combination of alleles for this gene. For each combination, state whether the plant would be **tall** or **short** and whether it is **homozygous dominant, heterozygous** or **homozygous recessive.**

**a)** ..............................................................................................................................................................................

**b)** ..............................................................................................................................................................................

**c)** ..............................................................................................................................................................................

**4** State whether the following combinations of genes are **homozygous dominant**, **heterozygous** or **homozygous recessive**.

**a)** Tt ........................................................... **b)** BB ...............................................................

**c)** ee ........................................................... **d)** Bb ...............................................................

## Monohybrid Inheritance and Inheritance of Eye-Colour

**1 a)** Complete these two different crosses between a brown-eyed and a blue-eyed parent.

**i)** Brown Eyes x Blue Eyes

**ii)** Brown Eyes x Blue Eyes

**Parents:**    BB    ×    bb            Bb    ×    bb

**Gametes:**    B        B    b        b        B        b    b        b

**Offspring:**

**Colour:** ...........................................................................................................................................................................................

**b)** For each of the crosses in part a), what is the percentage chance of a child having blue eyes?

**i)** ........................................................................    **ii)** ........................................................................

**2** Explain how two parents with brown eyes could produce children with blue eyes. Use a diagram to help.

...........................................................................................................

...........................................................................................................

...........................................................................................................

...........................................................................................................

...........................................................................................................

**3** Put a tick alongside the definition that best describes monohybrid inheritance.

**a)** Monohybrid inheritance occurs when a characteristic is controlled by several genes working together.    ☐

**b)** Monohybrid inheritance occurs when a characteristic is controlled by multiple alleles.    ☐

**c)** Monohybrid inheritance occurs when a characteristic is determined by a single gene, i.e. one pair of alleles.    ☐

# Biology Unit 2

## Differentiation of Cells

**1** Use the words provided to complete this passage about differentiation.

All of the cells in a living ............................ start out the same. They then become ............................ . That

is to say, they develop a ............................ with special ............................, which helps them to perform

specific ............................ . This process is called ............................ .

| differentiation | features | specialised | organism | structure | functions |
|---|---|---|---|---|---|

**2** Stem cells are cells that have not yet differentiated.

**a)** Why does this make them ideal for certain medical applications?

............................................................................................................................................

**b)** Name two places where human stem cells can be found.

**i)** ............................................................  **ii)** ............................................................

**3** Use the words provided to complete this passage about genes.

A gene is a section of ............................, which acts as a code. This code provides ............................

for making a particular protein by determining the ............................ used and the ............................

in which they are joined. The resulting proteins control how the individual ............................ functions

and how the ............................ as a whole develops.

| sequence | organism | instructions | cell | DNA | amino acids |
|---|---|---|---|---|---|

**4** Draw a diagram to show all the possible outcomes of a cross between a mother who is heterozygous for Huntington's disease (Hh) and a father who is healthy (hh).

# How Science Works

**To answer the questions on this page, you will have to recall scientific facts and draw upon your knowledge of how science works, e.g. scientific procedures, issues and ideas.**

**1** In the late 19th Century, Gregor Mendel observed that in pea plants there were just two possible outcomes for height: tall or dwarf.

His experiments led him to identify 'determiners', which we now know to be genes.

In his initial experiments Mendel crossed a pure-breeding tall plant with a pure-breeding dwarf plant, producing offspring that were all tall.

**a)** If the height of pea plants is determined by a single gene…

   **i)** which characteristic is dominant? _____

   **ii)** which characteristic is recessive? _____

**b)** Draw a genetic diagram to illustrate this cross. Use T for the dominant characteristic and t for the recessive one.

**c)** In his second stage of experiments, Mendel crossed two of the offspring from his initial experiments. In the resulting offspring, there was one dwarf plant for every three tall plants. Draw a genetic diagram to illustrate this cross.

**d)** Mendel used over 21 000 plants in his experiments. Explain why it was important for him to perform the same experiments using lots of different plants.

_____

_____

_____

# How Science Works

**To answer the questions on this page, you will have to recall scientific facts and draw upon your knowledge of how science works, e.g. scientific procedures, issues and ideas.**

**1 a)** Why do some people believe that embryos should be treated like people?

**b)** Why do others disagree?

**c)** Which group do you think is most likely to disagree with stem cells being extracted from embryos for medical purposes?

**2** For people with certain diseases, stem cell therapy could provide relief from symptoms and extend their life expectancy.

**a)** In terms of the patient's quality of life, what effect do you think this will have?

**b)** In terms of population size, what effect do you think this will have?

**c)** Suggest two ways in which this might impact on society. (Hint: think about things like housing and employment.)

**i)**

**ii)**

**3 a)** Most of the embryos used in stem cell research are left over from IVF treatments. How are these embryos produced?

**b)** With reference to Question 1, why do you think it is important to get a couple's consent before using their embryos for stem cell research?

# How Science Works

**To answer the questions on this page, you will have to recall scientific facts and draw upon your knowledge of how science works, e.g. scientific procedures, issues and ideas.**

**HT**

**1** If it became common practice to screen embryos for 'faulty' genes and abort those with defects, certain diseases and disorders could eventually be completely eliminated.

**a)** Below are some of the arguments for and against this practice. Write **for** or **against** alongside each one.

**i)** The money that is currently spent treating these diseases could be put to use elsewhere. _____

**ii)** Disease is a natural way of controlling the population size. _____

**iii)** It would devalue the lives of people currently living with disease. _____

**iv)** It would prevent unnecessary pain and suffering. _____

**v)** An embryo is a new life; destroying it is murder. _____

**vi)** It would free up hospital beds and resources for other patients. _____

**b)** Select one argument that is concerned with economics (i.e. money).

_____

**c)** Select one argument that is concerned with society (i.e. the overall impact on the population).

_____

**d)** Select one argument that is concerned with ethics (i.e. what is morally accepted).

_____

**2** There are concerns that people might start using genetic screening methods to select the sex and characteristics of their children.

**a)** Give one ethical argument against this.

_____

**b)** In terms of variation, explain how this could affect the population.

_____

_____

_____

# How Science Works

**To answer the questions on this page, you will have to recall scientific facts and draw upon your knowledge of how science works, e.g. scientific procedures, issues and ideas.**

**HT**

**1** Cystic fibrosis is an inherited disorder caused by a recessive allele.

**a)** Draw a diagram to show all the possible outcomes of a cross between a mother who has cystic fibrosis (cc) and a father who does not (CC).

**b)** What is the percentage chance that their offspring will be heterozygous for the disorder?

**c)** With the aid of a diagram, explain how a couple, neither of whom have cystic fibrosis, could have a child with cystic fibrosis.

# Biology Unit 2 - Key Words

**1** Alongside each of the following definitions, write the word being described.

**a)** A catalyst that increases the rate of biochemical reactions (6).

**b)** A collection of similar cells which work together to perform a function (6).

**c)** A collection of tissues which work together to perform a particular function (5).

**d)** A fluid-filled sac found inside plant cells (7).

**e)** A fundamental unit of a living organism (4).

**f)** A specialised sex cell (6).

**g)** A substance that increases the rate of a chemical reaction (8).

**h)** Will not dissolve; a property (9).

**i)** A toxin produced when proteins are broken down (4).

**j)** Allows substances to pass through (9).

**k)** An alternative form of a gene (6).

**l)** An enzyme that breaks down fat into fatty acids and glycerol (6).

**m)** An enzyme that breaks down starch (7).

**n)** An enzyme used to break down proteins (8).

**o)** Developed for a specific function (11).

**p)** Natural decomposition (5).

**q)** Respiration in the absence of oxygen (9).

**r)** Respiration using oxygen (7).

**s)** The ability to dissolve (7).

**t)** The automatic movement of particles along a concentration gradient (9).

**u)** The automatic movement of water along a concentration gradient (7).

**v)** The division of a cell, to form two daughter cells with the same number of chromosomes as the parent (7).

**w)** The division of a parent cell to form two daughter cells with half its number of chromosomes (7).

**x)** The fusion of a male gamete with a female gamete (13).

**y)** The greenish-yellow liquid produced by the liver (4).

**z)** The main operating temperature of an organism (4).

**aa)** The maintenance of a constant body temperature (16).

**bb)** The mass of living material in an organism (7) .

**cc)** The measure of acidity (2).

**dd)** The narrowest type of blood vessel (9).

**ee)** The part of a cell involved in protein synthesis (9).

**ff)** The part of a plant cell that contains chlorophyll (11)

**gg)** The pigment found in green plants responsible for photosynthesis (11).

**hh)** The process by which plants produce glucose using light energy (14).

**ii)** The soft tissue found inside bones (6).

**jj)** The substance from which chromosomes are made (3).

**kk)** The substance outside the nucleus of a cell, in which the organelles are suspended (9).

**ll)** The waste product produced by the kidneys (5).

**mm)** Very small organisms, often single cells (13).

# Chemistry Unit 2

## Subatomic Particles

**1 a)** Complete the table about atomic particles.

| Atomic Particle | Relative Charge |
| --- | --- |
| .......................................................... | +1 |
| .......................................................... | .......................................................... |
| Electron | .......................................................... |

**b)** Describe the structure of an atom in terms of these particles.

..............................................................................................................

..............................................................................................................

..............................................................................................................

**2 a)** Protons, neutrons and electrons have relative electrical charges. Explain briefly why atoms of a particular element have no overall charge.

..............................................................................................................

..............................................................................................................

**b)** Atoms of different elements have different numbers of protons. What is the number of protons in an atom otherwise known as?

..............................................................................................................

**c) i)** What does electron configuration tell us?

..............................................................................................................

..............................................................................................................

**ii)** The electron configuration of aluminium is 2, 8, 3. Briefly describe below what these numbers mean.

..............................................................................................................

..............................................................................................................

..............................................................................................................

## Electronic Structure

**1** How are elements arranged in the periodic table?

## The Alkali Metals (Group 1)

**2 a)** Why do all of the elements in Group 1 have similar properties?

**b)** What is produced when they react with non-metal elements?

## The Halogens (Group 7)

**3 a)** Why do all of the elements in Group 7 have similar properties?

**b)** What is produced when they react with alkali metals?

## Compounds and Mixtures

**4 a)** I consist of two or more elements or compounds that are not chemically combined together. The properties of the substances remain unchanged and specific to that substance. What am I?

**b)** We are substances in which the atoms of two or more elements are chemically combined (not just mixed together). What are we?

**5** What are the two ways in which atoms can form chemical bonds?

**a)**

**b)**

# Chemistry Unit 2

## The Ionic Bond

**1** Calcium and chlorine react together to produce calcium chloride. The equation for this reaction is:

$$Ca + Cl_2 \longrightarrow CaCl_2$$

**a)** Use the periodic table at the back of this book to find the atomic numbers for calcium and chlorine.

**i)** ........................................................  **ii)** ........................................................

**b)** Draw electron configuration diagrams for **i)** a calcium atom and **ii)** a chlorine atom.

**i)** Calcium (2,8,8,2)

**ii)** Chlorine (2,8,7)

**c)** Calcium chloride is an ionic compound. Explain how…

**i)** a calcium atom becomes a calcium ion.

........................................................................................................................................................................

**ii)** a chlorine atom becomes a chloride ion.

........................................................................................................................................................................

**d)** Draw an electron configuration diagram of calcium chloride ($CaCl_2$).

**2** Calcium also reacts with oxygen to form calcium oxide ($CaO$). Explain how the ionic bond is formed between calcium and oxygen to produce this compound.

........................................................................................................................................................................

........................................................................................................................................................................

........................................................................................................................................................................

## The Covalent Bond

**1** What, exactly, is a covalent bond?

_____

_____

**2** The diagram represents a molecule of hydrogen chloride. It is a gas at room temperature.

**a)** What type of particles are represented by the...

**i)** Dot (●)? _____ **ii)** Crosses (**X**)? _____

**b)** Explain why hydrogen chloride is a gas at room temperature.

_____

**3** Nitrogen gas always exists as molecules made up of pairs of atoms represented by $N_2$. Nitrogen atoms have five electrons in their outer shells.

**a)** Draw two separate nitrogen atoms.

**b)** Draw a pair of nitrogen atoms 'joined' to form an $N_2$ molecule.

| **a)** | **b)** |
| --- | --- |
|  |  |
|  |  |

**c)** What sort of bond exists between the pair of atoms in part b)?

_____

**d)** Which are stronger – the bonds between nitrogen atoms within an $N_2$ molecule, or the bonds between $N_2$ molecules?

_____

# Chemistry Unit 2

## Covalent Bonding

**4** Bromine atoms join together to form bromine molecules.

**a)** What is the name of the bond formed between the bromine atoms in a bromine molecule?

**b)** This bond can be represented in three ways, as shown in the table below. Complete the table drawing similar diagrams for the other substances listed. Use the periodic table at the back of this book to help you.

| Substance | Formula | Structural Formulae | | |
|-----------|---------|------|------|------|
| | | **i)** | **ii)** | **iii)** |
| Bromine | $Br_2$ | Br - Br | Br    Br | Br Br |
| Chlorine | $Cl_2$ | | | |
| Oxygen | $O_2$ | | | |
| Ammonia | $NH_3$ | | | |
| Hydrogen | $H_2$ | | | |
| Water | $H_2O$ | | | |
| Methane | $CH_4$ | | | |

## Giant Covalent Structures

**1** The diagrams below show two giant structures of carbon.

**i)**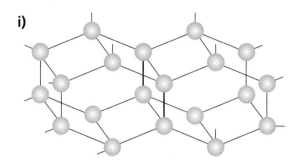

**ii)**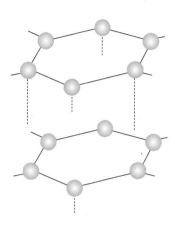

**a)** Which structure is **graphite** and which structure is **diamond**?

**i)** ........................................................ **ii)** ........................................

**b)** Complete the following explanations:

**i)** Diamond has a very high melting point, because...

.................................................................................................................

.................................................................................................................

**ii)** Graphite can be used as a lubricant, because...

.................................................................................................................

.................................................................................................................

**2 a)** Silica ($SiO_2$) is a 'pure form' of sand. Explain why it has a very high melting point.

.................................................................................................................

**b)** Describe how the atoms in silica are bonded to each other.

.................................................................................................................

.................................................................................................................

**HT**

**3** Explain how the structure of metals allows them to conduct heat and electricity.

.................................................................................................................

.................................................................................................................

.................................................................................................................

# Chemistry Unit 2

## Nanoparticles and Nanostructures

**1** **a)** What is nanoscience the study of?

_____

**b)** One nanometre is 0.000000001m – one billionth of a metre. How else can this be written?

_____

**c)** Briefly describe the recent developments that have allowed scientists to see and control atoms at this dimension.

_____

_____

_____

_____

**d)** List two ways in which nanoparticles show different properties to the same materials in bulk.

**i)** _____

**ii)** _____

## Nanocomposites

**2** A lot of work has been done recently in the area of nanocomposite materials.

**a)** How do nanocomposite polymers differ from ordinary plastics?

_____

**b)** List four uses of nanocomposite materials.

**i)** _____

**ii)** _____

**iii)** _____

**iv)** _____

To answer the questions on this page, you will have to recall scientific facts and draw upon your knowledge of how science works, e.g. scientific procedures, issues and ideas.

**1** Complete Column 3 of the table below, giving at least two uses for each example. The first box has been completed for you.

| Substance | Properties | Uses |
|---|---|---|
| Metal | Strong / Shiny / Good conductor of heat and electricity / Malleable (bendy). | Construction, Jewellery, Pans, Wires, Pipes |
| Non-metal | Brittle / Insulators. | |
| Polymer | Lightweight / Flexible / Waterproof. | |
| Ionic compound | Hard, crystalline, soluble in water / High melting points / Insulators when solid but conduct electricity when molten or dissolved. | |
| Molecular covalent | Soft / Low melting points / Insulators. | |
| Macromolecules | Hard / High melting points. | |
| Nanomaterial | Very strong / Huge surface area / Conduct electricity. | |
| Smart material | Shape memory. | |

**2** Nanomaterials have many applications, but give one disadvantage of using them.

# Chemistry Unit 2

## Mass Number and Atomic Number

**1** In the nucleus of a potassium atom there are 19 protons and 20 neutrons.

**a)** What is the mass number of potassium?

........................................................................................................................................

**b)** What is the atomic number of potassium?

........................................................................................................................................

**c)** How many electrons does an atom of potassium contain?

........................................................................................................................................

**d)** Why is an atom of potassium neutral in terms of electric charge?

........................................................................................................................................

**2 a)** The letters A, B, C, D, E, F and G below represent seven different elements.

For each one write down **i)** their atomic number **ii)** their mass number **iii)** the number of protons and **iv)** the number of neutrons in one atom (A, B, C, D, E, F and G are not their chemical symbols).

| | $^{12}_{6}A$ | $^{9}_{4}B$ | $^{19}_{9}C$ | $^{11}_{5}D$ | $^{25}_{14}E$ | $^{40}_{18}F$ | $^{35}_{17}G$ |
|---|---|---|---|---|---|---|---|
| **i)** Atomic Number | | | | | | | |
| **ii)** Mass Number | | | | | | | |
| **iii)** No. of Protons | | | | | | | |
| **iv)** No. of Neutrons | | | | | | | |

**b)** Use the periodic table at the back of this book to identify the elements A, B, C, D, E, F and G.

A= ........................................        B= ........................................        C= ........................................        D= ........................................

E= ........................................        F= ........................................        G= ........................................

## Mass Number and Atomic Number

**3** Complete the following table. The first one has been done for you.

| | $^{14}_{7}\text{N}$ | $^{197}_{79}\text{Au}$ | $^{235}_{92}\text{U}$ | Ca | $^{84}_{36}$ | 226 | $_{30}$ | Fe |
|---|---|---|---|---|---|---|---|---|
| No. of Protons | 7 | | | 20 | | | | 26 |
| No. of Neutrons | 7 | | | 20 | | | 34 | 30 |
| No. of Electrons | 7 | | | | | 88 | | |
| Element | Nitrogen | | | | Krypton | | | |

## Isotopes

**4** What do we mean by the term 'isotope'?

**5** The following show symbol representations of two isotopes of hydrogen.

i) $^{1}_{1}\text{H}$     ii) $^{2}_{1}\text{H}$

**a)** How do we know that they are isotopes of hydrogen?

**b)** How many electrons would isotope i) contain?

**c)** How many neutrons would isotope ii) contain?

**d)** Do isotopes have an electrical charge? Explain your answer.

# Chemistry Unit 2

## Relative Formula Mass ($M_r$)

**1** Calculate the relative formula mass of the following compounds (the periodic table at the back of this book will be useful).

**a)** Water, $H_2O$ _____

**b)** Sodium Chloride, NaCl _____

**c)** Copper Oxide, CuO _____

**d)** Aluminium Oxide, $Al_2O_3$ _____

**e)** Copper Sulfate, $CuSO_4$ _____

**f)** Calcium Hydroxide, $Ca(OH)_2$ _____

**g)** Aluminium Chloride, $AlCl_3$ _____

**h)** Sulfuric Acid, $H_2SO_4$ _____

**i)** Ethene, $C_2H_4$ _____

**j)** Sodium Carbonate, $Na_2CO_3$ _____

**k)** Aluminium Sulfate, $Al_2(SO_4)_3$ _____

**l)** Ammonia, $NH_3$ _____

**2** For each of the following compounds 'X' is an unknown element. The relative formula mass of the compound is given in brackets. Work out which element X represents.

**a)** $XO(40)$ _____

**b)** $XCl_2(110)$ _____

**c)** $CX_2(44)$ _____

**d)** $XNO_3(63)$ _____

**e)** $X_2(62)$ _____

**f)** $MgX_2(94)$ _____

**g)** $X(OH)_2(171)$ _____

**h)** $X_2O_3(188)$ _____

## Relative Atomic Mass ($A_r$)

**3** Use the periodic table at the back of this book to find out the relative atomic mass of the following elements:

**a)** Beryllium _____

**b)** Aluminium _____

**c)** Chlorine _____

**d)** Titanium _____

**e)** Bromine _____

**f)** Argon _____

**g)** Tellurium _____

**h)** Lithium _____

**i)** Tungsten _____

**j)** Francium _____

**k)** Nitrogen _____

**l)** Boron _____

## Calculating Percentage Mass of an Element in a Compound

**1** Using the periodic table at the back of this book, calculate the percentage mass of the given element in each of the compounds below.

**a)** Oxygen, O, in Calcium Oxide, CaO

**b)** Chlorine, Cl, in Sodium Chloride, NaCl

**c)** Calcium, Ca, in Calcium Carbonate, $CaCO_3$

**d)** Sulfur, S, in Sulfur Dioxide, $SO_2$

HT

**2 a)** Use the periodic table at the back of this book to find the relative atomic mass of...

**i)** Hydrogen

**ii)** Sulfur

**iii)** Oxygen

**b)** Calculate the empirical formula of the compound formed by reacting 0.04g of hydrogen, 0.64g of sulfur and 1.28g of oxygen. Show your working.

Empirical Formula:

# Chemistry Unit 2

## The Mole

**1** What do we mean by the term 'mole' (mol)?

_____

_____

**2** Use the periodic table at the back of this book to answer the following questions:

**a)** What is the molar mass (g/mol) of the following elements?

**i)** Calcium

_____

**ii)** Aluminium

_____

**b)** What is the mass (g) of one mole of the following compounds?

**i)** Sodium hydroxide (NaOH)

_____

**ii)** Sulfur dioxide ($SO_2$)

_____

**3 a)** What is the relationship used to calculate questions involving moles?

_____

**b)** Use the relationship and the periodic table at the back of this book to calculate…

**i)** the number of moles of calcium in 120g of the element.

Answer: _____

_____

**ii)** the number of moles of calcium carbonate ($CaCO_3$) in 500g of the compound.

Answer: _____

_____

HT

## Calculating the Mass of a Product

**1** Calcium carbonate and hydrochloric acid react together to produce calcium chloride, carbon dioxide and water. Below is the balanced symbol equation for this reaction.

$$CaCO_3(s) + 2HCl(aq) \longrightarrow CaCl_2(aq) + CO_2(g) + H_2O(l)$$

**a)** Work out the $M_r$ for each of the reactants and products shown in the equation and write them below.

**i)** $CaCO_3$ _____        **ii)** $2HCl$ _____        **iii)** $CaCl_2$ _____

**iv)** $CO_2$ _____        **v)** $H_2O$ _____

**b)** What is the total mass of all the reactants in the equation?

_____

**c)** What is the total mass of all the products in the equation?

_____

**d)** Would you have expected the masses in part b) and c) to be the same? Explain your answer.

_____

**e)** What mass of calcium chloride can be produced from 2 grams of calcium carbonate?

_____

_____

_____

_____

## Calculating the Mass of a Reactant

**2** Referring to the equation in Question 1, how much calcium carbonate is needed to produce 1kg (1000g) of calcium chloride?

_____

_____

_____

_____

# Chemistry Unit 2

## Calculating the Percentage Yield

**1** Give three reasons why it is not always possible to obtain the full, calculated mass of a product from a reaction.

a) ........................................................................................................................................

b) ........................................................................................................................................

c) ........................................................................................................................................

**HT**

**2 a)** What is the actual quantity of product obtained through a reaction called?

........................................................................................................................................

**b)** Write down the word equation that relates the actual amount of product obtained to the maximum amount of product that could theoretically be obtained.

**3** The reaction for making ammonia from hydrogen and nitrogen gas is shown by the following equation:

$$3H_2 + N_2 \longrightarrow 2NH_3$$

The industrial process for making ammonia produces 5.1 tonnes of ammonia from 6 tonnes of hydrogen gas. Calculate the percentage yield of this process.

........................................................................................................................................

........................................................................................................................................

........................................................................................................................................

## Calculating Atom Economy

**4 a)** What is meant by the term 'atom economy'?

........................................................................................................................................

........................................................................................................................................

**b)** What equation is used for calculating atom economy?

........................................................................................................................................

## Reversible Reactions

**1** Some chemical reactions are reversible.

**a)** Explain how a reaction can be reversible.

_____

**b)** Write the symbol that is used in equations to show that a reaction is reversible.

_____

## Production of Ammonia - the Haber Process

**2 a)** The Haber Process is used to make ammonia. Complete this flow diagram of the process by filling in the spaces.

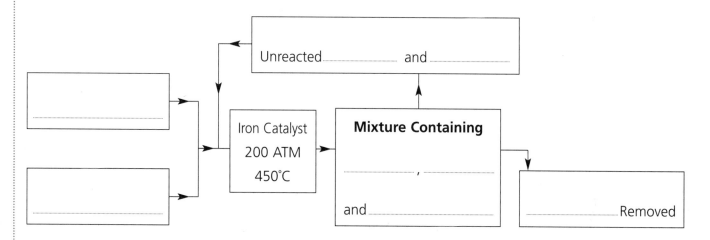

**b)** Write a word equation for the reaction (remember that the reaction is reversible!).

_____

**c)** Convert this to a balanced symbol equation, with state symbols.

_____

**d)** Where are the following raw materials obtained?

**i)** Nitrogen: _____

**ii)** Hydrogen: _____

# How Science Works

**To answer the questions on this page, you will have to recall scientific facts and draw upon your knowledge of how science works, e.g. scientific procedures, issues and ideas.**

**1** **a)** Write a short definition for….

   **i)** the relative atomic mass ($A_r$) of an element?

   ...........................................................................................................................................

   ...........................................................................................................................................

   ...........................................................................................................................................

   **ii)** the relative formula mass ($M_r$) of a compound?

   ...........................................................................................................................................

   ...........................................................................................................................................

   ...........................................................................................................................................

**2** Write the word equation used to calculate atom economy.

**Atom Economy =**

**3** Sodium ethanoate has many industrial applications. For example, it is used in the production of some dyed textiles and leather goods. It is a product of the following reaction:

Ethanoic acid + Sodium Carbonate ⟶ Sodium ethanoate + Carbon dioxide + Water

$$C_2H_4O_2 + Na_2CO_3 \longrightarrow C_2H_3NaO_2 + CO_2 + H_2O$$

**a)** Calculate the atom economy of this reaction. You will need to balance the equation first.

...........................................................................................................................................

...........................................................................................................................................

...........................................................................................................................................

...........................................................................................................................................

**b)** What is the percentage of waste products in this reaction?

...........................................................................................................................................

## Rates of Reactions

**1 a)** What is the term used to describe the minimum amount of energy required to cause a chemical reaction?

_____

**b)** What are the four main factors which affect the rate of reaction?

**i)** _____

**ii)** _____

**iii)** _____

**iv)** _____

## Temperature of the Reactants

**2** The word equation below shows the reaction between lumps of calcium carbonate and hydrochloric acid.

Calcium carbonate + Hydrochloric acid ⟶ Calcium chloride + Water + Carbon dioxide

The rate of reaction can be studied by measuring the amount of carbon dioxide gas produced. The graph shows the result of four experiments: A, B, C and D. For each experiment only the temperature of the acid was changed.

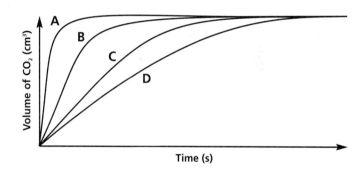

**a)** What should have been kept constant in order to make this experiment a fair test?

_____

**b)** Which graph line shows the results of the experiment with the acid at the highest temperature?

_____

**c)** Explain your answer to part b) fully in terms of the particles involved.

_____

_____

# Chemistry Unit 2

## Concentration of the Dissolved Reactants

**3** A student carried out an experiment where hydrochloric acid was reacted with sodium thiosulfate. In this reaction a yellow precipitate of sulfur is formed. The rate of reaction can be measured by timing how long it takes a cross drawn under a flask to disappear from view. The results obtained are shown below.

| Concentration of Acid (M) | Time Taken for Cross to Disappear (s) |
|---|---|
| 0.1 | 60 |
| 0.2 | 40 |
| 0.4 | 24 |
| 0.6 | 13 |
| 0.8 | 8 |
| 1.0 | 4 |

**a)** Plot a graph of these results.

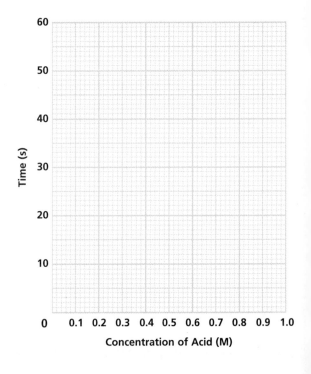

**b) i)** What happens to the rate of reaction as the concentration increases?

......................................................................................

**ii)** Explain your answer to part b) i) in terms of the particles involved.

......................................................................................

......................................................................................

**4** How are concentrations of solutions measured?

......................................................................................

**5 a)** What happens to the rate of reaction when the pressure on a gas increases?

......................................................................................

**b)** Explain your answer in terms of the particles involved.

......................................................................................

......................................................................................

## Surface Area of Solid Reactants

**6** Large particles have a small surface area in relation to their volume, and small particles have a large surface area in relation to their volume.

Explain how the size of the particles involved affects the rate of reaction.

_____

_____

_____

_____

## Using a Catalyst

**7** What is a catalyst?

_____

_____

**8** The word equation below shows the decomposition of hydrogen peroxide to give water and oxygen.

Hydrogen peroxide ⟶ Water + Oxygen

Adding manganese (IV) oxide speeds up this reaction without altering the products formed.

A student adds 2g of manganese (IV) oxide to 100cm³ of hydrogen peroxide at 20°C. He measures the volume of oxygen produced over a period of five minutes. The results are shown:

| Time (mins) | 0 | 1 | 2 | 3 | 4 | 5 |
|---|---|---|---|---|---|---|
| Total Volume of Oxygen (cm³) | 0 | 54 | 82 | 96 | 100 | 100 |

**a)** Suggest what the total volume of oxygen would be after 6 minutes. Explain your answer.

_____

_____

**b)** Explain how manganese (IV) oxide increases the rate of the reaction.

_____

# Chemistry Unit 2

## Analysing the Rate of Reaction

**1** **a)** What two measurements are needed to find the rate of a chemical reaction?

i) .................................................................................................................................

ii) .................................................................................................................................

**b)** Write the general equation that can be used to calculate the rate of reaction.

...........................................................................................................................................

...........................................................................................................................................

**2** The graph below shows the results of an investigation into the reaction of magnesium with dilute hydrochloric acid.

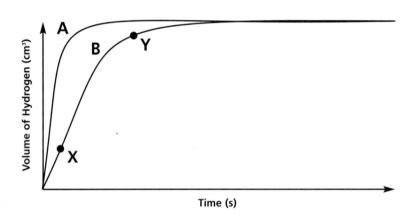

**a)** Complete the word equation for the reaction.

Magnesium + Hydrochloric Acid ⟶ ................................................ + Hydrogen

**b)** Which graph line shows the fastest rate of reaction?

...........................................................................................................................................

**c)** For Graph B, is the rate of reaction greatest at X or Y?

...........................................................................................................................................

**d)** Give three possible reasons why the rate of reaction is different for Graphs A and B.

i) .................................................................................................................................

ii) .................................................................................................................................

iii) .................................................................................................................................

**To answer the questions on this page, you will have to recall scientific facts and draw upon your knowledge of how science works, e.g. scientific procedures, issues and ideas.**

**1** What four factors affect the rate of reaction?

**a)** ......................................................................................................................................

**b)** ......................................................................................................................................

**c)** ......................................................................................................................................

**d)** ......................................................................................................................................

**2** The decomposition of hydrogen peroxide to give water and oxygen is shown below as a word equation.

Hydrogen peroxide ⟶ Water + Oxygen

A student adds 2g of manganese (IV) oxide (a catalyst) to 100cm³ of hydrogen peroxide at 20°C. He measured the volume of oxygen produced over a period of five minutes. The results are shown alongside.

| Time (mins) | 0 | 1 | 2 | 3 | 4 | 5 |
|---|---|---|---|---|---|---|
| Total Volume of Oxygen (cm³) | 0 | 54 | 82 | 96 | 100 | 100 |

**a)** Plot the results on the graph paper alongside. Label this Graph A.

**b)** The student repeats the experiment. This time he adds 2g of manganese oxide to a mixture of 50cm³ of hydrogen peroxide and 50cm³ of water at 20°C.

**i)** On the same axes, sketch the graph that you would expect if all other conditions were kept the same as in the first experiment. Label this Graph B.

**ii)** Briefly explain the difference between Graphs A and B.

......................................................................................................................

......................................................................................................................

......................................................................................................................

......................................................................................................................

# How Science Works

**To answer the questions on this page, you will have to recall scientific facts and draw upon your knowledge of how science works, e.g. scientific procedures, issues and ideas.**

**1** Why can catalysts be used over and over again?

.......................................................................................................................................................................

.......................................................................................................................................................................

**2** List three transition materials that are used as catalysts in industrial processes.

**a)** ...............................................................................................................................................................

**b)** ...............................................................................................................................................................

**c)** ...............................................................................................................................................................

**3** Why are nanomaterials ideal for use as industrial catalysts?

.......................................................................................................................................................................

**4** **a)** List three advantages of using catalysts in industrial processes.

**i)** ...........................................................................................................................................................

**ii)** ..........................................................................................................................................................

**iii)** .........................................................................................................................................................

**b)** List two disadvantages of using catalysts in industrial processes.

**i)** ...........................................................................................................................................................

**ii)** ..........................................................................................................................................................

**5** Use the library, Internet or another secondary source to find one example of a catalyst being used effectively in industry. Summarise your findings below.

.......................................................................................................................................................................

.......................................................................................................................................................................

.......................................................................................................................................................................

.......................................................................................................................................................................

.......................................................................................................................................................................

## Exothermic Reactions

**1** Methane reacts with oxygen to produce carbon dioxide and water.

**a)** Write a word equation for this reaction.

...........................................................................................................................................................

**b)** What else is produced in addition to the products mentioned in this question?

...........................................................................................................................................................

**c)** What is the name given to this type of reaction?

...........................................................................................................................................................

**2** In an exothermic reaction, what happens to the yield if the temperature...

**a)** rises? ..........................................         **b)** lowers? ..........................................

## Endothermic Reactions

**3** When ammonium chloride is dissolved in water an endothermic reaction takes place.

**a)** What do we mean by an endothermic reaction?

...........................................................................................................................................................

**b)** In an endothermic reaction, what happens to the yield if the temperature...

**i)** rises? ..........................................         **ii)** lowers? ..........................................

**4 a)** What substance is produced when hydrated copper sulfate crystals are gently heated?

...........................................................................................................................................................

**b)** The change is reversible. What does this mean?

...........................................................................................................................................................

**c)** Would the reverse reaction be endothermic or exothermic?

...........................................................................................................................................................

## Reversible Reactions

**1** The diagram shows an experiment where ammonium chloride is heated.

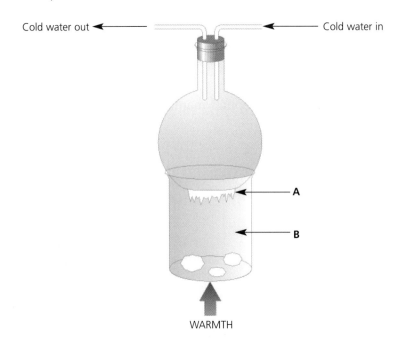

The word equation for the reaction is:

**Ammonium chloride ⇌ Ammonia + Hydrogen Chloride**

**a)** What does the symbol ⇌ mean?

......................................................................................................................................................

**b)** Explain why…

**i)** ammonium chloride is found at point A.

......................................................................................................................................................

......................................................................................................................................................

**ii)** ammonia and hydrogen chloride gas are found in the beaker at point B.

......................................................................................................................................................

......................................................................................................................................................

**c)** Write a symbol equation for this reaction.

......................................................................................................................................................

## Reversible Reactions in Closed Systems

**1** In the Haber Process two gases, nitrogen and hydrogen, react together to produce ammonia in a reversible reaction. The table below shows how the yield of ammonia changes at different temperatures and pressures.

The symbol equation is: $N_{2(g)} + 3H_{2(g)} \rightleftharpoons 2NH_{3(g)}$

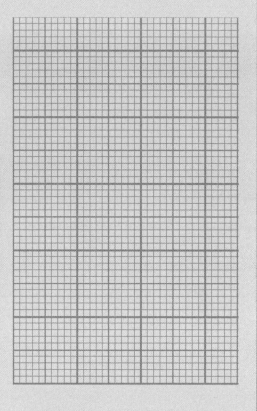

| Pressure (atmospheres) | Percentage Yield of Ammonia at 300°C | Percentage Yield of Ammonia at 600°C |
|---|---|---|
| 100 | 43 | 4 |
| 200 | 62 | 12 |
| 300 | 74 | 18 |
| 400 | 79 | 19 |
| 500 | 80 | 20 |

**a)** Plot a graph of the data above.

**b)** Is this an endothermic or exothermic reaction?

_____

**c) i)** Explain why the yield of ammonia is affected by increasing the pressure at a constant temperature.

_____

_____

**ii)** Explain how the yield of ammonia is affected by decreasing the temperature at a constant pressure.

_____

_____

_____

**d)** To reach equilibrium the gases must be in a closed system. Why is this?

_____

# Chemistry Unit 2

**HT**

## Effect of Varying Conditions on Reversible Reactions

**1** **a)** In the Haber Process a mixture of nitrogen and hydrogen is passed over iron at a temperature of about 450° and a pressure of 200 atmospheres.

**i)** Write down a word and symbol equation for the reaction

_____

**ii)** Explain why the nitrogen and hydrogen are passed over iron.

_____

**b)** The graph alongside shows how temperature and pressure affect the % yield of ammonia in the reaction.

**i)** From looking at the graph, which combination of temperature and pressure gives the highest yield?

_____

_____

**ii)** Why is this combination of temperature and pressure not used in the commercial production of ammonia?

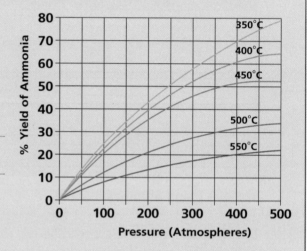

_____

_____

## A Compromise Solution

**2** **a)** Why is ammonia produced at a temperature of 450°C and a pressure of 200 atmospheres?

_____

**b)** From looking at the graph above, what yield does this combination of temperature and pressure give?

_____

**c)** What happens to the hydrogen and nitrogen that has not reacted to produce ammonia?

_____

**To answer the questions on this page, you will have to recall scientific facts and draw upon your knowledge of how science works, e.g. scientific procedures, issues and ideas.**

**1** **a)** Why do energy requirements need to be considered when using chemical reactions in industrial processes?

................................................................................................................................

................................................................................................................................

................................................................................................................................

**b)** With reference to chemical reactions being used in industrial processes, name one other factor that needs to be considered that can affect...

**i)** how economical a process is.

................................................................................................................................

**ii)** how environmentally friendly the process is.

................................................................................................................................

**2** **a)** What two main variables affect the speed of a chemical reaction in an industrial process?

**i)** ...........................................................    **ii)** ...........................................................

**b)** List two advantages and two disadvantages for variable i) above.

ADVANTAGES    **i)** ................................................................................................

    **ii)** ................................................................................................

DISADVANTAGES  **iii)** ................................................................................................

    **iv)** ................................................................................................

**c)** List two advantages and two disadvantages for variable ii) in part a) above.

ADVANTAGES    **i)** ................................................................................................

    **ii)** ................................................................................................

DISADVANTAGES  **iii)** ................................................................................................

    **iv)** ................................................................................................

# Chemistry Unit 2

## Principles of Electrolysis

**1** What are ionic substances?

_____

_____

_____

**2** In terms of elements and ions, explain what electrolysis is.

_____

_____

_____

**3** **a)** Fill in the type of charge (i.e. **positive** or **negative**) to complete these two sentences, which describe what happens during electrolysis.

    **i)** Ions with a _____ charge move towards the positive electrode.

    **ii)** Ions with a _____ charge move towards the negative electrode.

  **b)** If there is a mixture of ions in a solution during electrolysis, what is the formation of the products dependent on?

_____

_____

**4** What two elements would be produced through the electrolysis of copper chloride solution? Use state symbols to indicate the state of these products.

  **a) i)** Element: _____      **ii)** State Symbol: _____

  **b) i)** Element: _____      **ii)** State Symbol: _____

## Redox Reactions

**5** Alongside each statement below, write whether the process being described is a **reduction** or **oxidation**.

  **a)** Positively charged ions gain electrons. _____

  **b)** Negatively charged ions lose electrons. _____

**6** Complete this mnemonic to help you remember what occurs in a redox reaction.

  **a)** O _____    I _____    L _____

  **b)** R _____    I _____    G _____

## Purification of Copper by Electrolysis

**1** Copper which is used for electrical wiring must be very pure. Pure copper can be made by electrolysis. The diagram alongside shows a very simple arrangement.

**a)** For the electrolysis of copper to take place, what must the solution in the cell contain?

..................................................................................................................................................................................

**b)** Which electrode should be made of impure copper? ........................................................................................

**c)** Which electrode should be made of pure copper? ...........................................................................................

**d)** Which electrode increases in size during electrolysis? ..................................................................................

**e)** Which electrode decreases in size during electrolysis? ................................................................................

**f)** Explain, in terms of ions, why the two electrodes change in size during electrolysis.

..................................................................................................................................................................................

..................................................................................................................................................................................

..................................................................................................................................................................................

..................................................................................................................................................................................

**HT**

**2 a)** Write a half-equation to show what happens at the negative electrode during electrolysis.

..................................................................................................................................................................................

**b)** Write a half-equation to show what happens at the positive electrode during electrolysis.

..................................................................................................................................................................................

# Chemistry Unit 2

## Industrial Electrolysis of Sodium Chloride Solution

**1** The diagram alongside shows the
arrangement for the electrolysis of
a solution of sodium chloride.

**a)** Why must sodium chloride be in solution for
electrolysis to take place?

Sodium
Chloride
Solution
NaCl

Positive
Electrode

Membrane

Negative
Electrode

........................................................................................

........................................................................................

........................................................................................

**b)** Name the gas formed at **i)** the negative electrode and **ii)** the positive electrode.

**i)** ...................................................................... **ii)** ......................................................................

**c)** Describe a test for the gas formed at the positive electrode.

........................................................................................................................................................

**d)** Apart from the two gases, what else is produced during the electrolysis of sodium chloride?

........................................................................................................................................................

**2** For each reagent produced, give one example of how it can be used commercially.

**a)** Reagent: ...................................... Use: ......................................................

**b)** Reagent: ...................................... Use: ......................................................

**c)** Reagent: ...................................... Use: ......................................................

## Indicators

**3 a)** What is an indicator?

........................................................................................................................................................

........................................................................................................................................................

**b)** Name two indicators.

**i)** ...................................................................... **ii)** ......................................................................

## Neutralisation

**1** A beaker containing 100cm³ of sodium hydroxide had universal indicator solution added to it. Sulfuric acid was then added using a burette and the pH of the solution was estimated by gauging the colour of the liquid. The solution was constantly stirred. The results are shown below.

| Volume of Acid Added (cm³) | 0 | 4 | 12 | 30 | 50 |
|---|---|---|---|---|---|
| pH of solution | 14 | 12 | 10 | 8 | 7 |

**a)** Plot a graph of these results.

**b)** What colour was the solution at the start?

**c)** What colour was the solution at the end?

**d)** Write a symbol equation for the reaction taking place.

**e)** What is the name given to this type of reaction?

**f)** Describe the reaction in terms of ions.

**g)** Write an equation for the reaction showing the ions that combine.

**2** Ammonium nitrate and ammonium sulfate can be used as fertilisers.

Ammonia is reacted with an acid in each case. Write word equations for the formation of...

**a)** Ammonium nitrate:

**b)** Ammonium sulfate:

# Chemistry Unit 2

## Soluble Salts from Metals

**1** **a)** Write a word equation for the general reaction that takes place between a metal and dilute acid.

**b)** Describe what is meant by the term 'salt'.

**c)** Indicate what happens when each of the metals alongside are reacted with an acid. The first one has been completed for you.

| Metal | Reaction |
|---|---|
| **i)** Zinc | Fairly reasonable |
| **ii)** Silver | |
| **iii)** Magnesium | |
| **iv)** Potassium | |

## Soluble Salts from Insoluble Bases

**2** What is the difference between a base and an alkali?

**3** Explain, using diagrams, how you would obtain crystals of the salt formed in the reaction between copper oxide and hydrochloric acid.

| STEP 1: | STEP 2: | STEP 3: |
|---|---|---|
| | | |

**4** The substance produced when ammonia is dissolved in water can be neutralised with acids to produce ammonium salts, which are important as alkalis.

What is the substance produced when ammonia is dissolved in water?

## Salts of Alkali Metals

**1 a)** To refresh your memory, write a word equation to summarise what happens in a neutralisation reaction.

**b)** Complete the word equations for the following reactions:

**i)** Iron Hydroxide + Sulfuric Acid $\longrightarrow$ _____ + Water

**ii)** _____ + _____ $\longrightarrow$ Calcium Sulfate + Water

**iii)** Potassium Hydroxide + _____ $\longrightarrow$ Potassium Nitrate + _____

**iv)** _____ + Hydrochloric Acid $\longrightarrow$ Sodium Chloride + _____

**v)** _____ + _____ $\longrightarrow$ Calcium Chloride + Water

**vi)** Copper Oxide + Hydrochloric Acid $\longrightarrow$ _____ + _____

**vii)** _____ + Nitric Acid $\longrightarrow$ Sodium Nitrate + _____

**viii)** _____ + _____ $\longrightarrow$ Sodium Sulfate + _____

**ix)** Zinc Oxide + Nitric Acid $\longrightarrow$ _____ + _____

**x)** Ammonia + _____ $\longrightarrow$ Ammonium Chloride + _____

## Insoluble Salts

**2 a)** How are insoluble salts made?

**b)** Describe one practical application of this process.

# How Science Works

**To answer the questions on this page, you will have to recall scientific facts and draw upon your knowledge of how science works, e.g. scientific procedures, issues and ideas.**

**1 a)** Under what circumstances can ionic substances conduct electricity and be broken down?

......................................................................................................................................................................

**b)** What process uses electrical energy to break down these substances?

......................................................................................................................................................................

**c)** What is another name given to **i)** the positive and **ii)** the negative electrode used in this process?

**i)** ...................................................................... **ii)** ......................................................................

**2** List the three main rules for predicting the results of electrolysing ionic solutions.

**a)** ...................................................................................................................................................

......................................................................................................................................................................

**b)** ...................................................................................................................................................

......................................................................................................................................................................

**c)** ...................................................................................................................................................

......................................................................................................................................................................

**HT**

**3** Through electrolysis, concentrated hydrochloric acid gives equal volumes of hydrogen and chlorine gas.

**Hydrochloric acid ⟶ Hydrogen + Chlorine**

Write and balance half-equations which represent the changes that occur at the two electrodes during this electrolysis.

**a) i)** Equation: ......................................................................................................................

   **ii)** At which electrode? ....................................................................................................

**b) i)** Equation: ......................................................................................................................

   **ii)** At which electrode? ....................................................................................................

**To answer the questions on this page, you will have to recall scientific facts and draw upon your knowledge of how science works, e.g. scientific procedures, issues and ideas. (continued)**

**4** **a)** Briefly explain the process of electrolysis.

**b)** Why is electrolysis important industrially?

**5** **a)** Write a word equation for the electrolysis of sea water or brine.

**b)** List three advantages associated with the process.

**i)**

**ii)**

**iii)**

**c)** List three disadvantages associated with the process.

**i)**

**ii)**

**iii)**

**d)** Using your lists of advantages and disadvantages, briefly evaluate the long-term impact of this process on the environment.

# How Science Works

**To answer the questions on this page, you will have to recall scientific facts and draw upon your knowledge of how science works, e.g. scientific procedures, issues and ideas.**

**1 a)** What are the two main groups of salts?

**i)** ................................................................ **ii)** ................................................

**b)** Complete the following sentences.

**i)** Insoluble salts are made from ....................................................................................................

**ii)** Two solutions of soluble salts can react to make ...............................................................

**2** List the five rules which define the solubility of salts.

**a)** ..............................................................................................................................................................

**b)** ..............................................................................................................................................................

**c)** ..............................................................................................................................................................

**d)** ..............................................................................................................................................................

**e)** ..............................................................................................................................................................

**3** Complete the following table:

| Acid | Salt Products |
|---|---|
| Hydrochloric acid | ................................ |
| ................................ | Sulfates |
| Nitric acid | ................................ |

**4 a)** Write **i)** a general word equation for the production of insoluble salts and **ii)** a specific word equation for the production of copper sulfate.

**i)** ..............................................................................................................................................................

**ii)** ..............................................................................................................................................................

**b)** Briefly explain how copper sulfate is produced.

..............................................................................................................................................................

..............................................................................................................................................................

..............................................................................................................................................................

..............................................................................................................................................................

# Chemistry Unit 2 - Key Words

**1** Alongside each definition, write the word or phrase that is being described.

**a) 4 letters**   **i)** A compound that has a pH value lower than 7

     **ii)** The molecular weight of a substance expressed in grams

     **iii)** The product of a chemical reaction between a base and an acid

**b) 5 letters**   The amount of a product obtained from a reaction

**c) 6 letters**   **i)** A compound that has a pH value higher than 7

     **ii)** A positively charged particle found in the nucleus of atoms

**d) 7 letters**   **i)** A neutrally charged particle found in the nucleus of atoms

     **ii)** The small central core of an atom

**e) 8 letters**   **i)** Elements in Group 7 of the periodic table

     **ii)** Inert, colourless gases (2 words)

     **iii)** A negatively charged particle found outside the nucleus of an atom

**f) 9 letters**   **i)** A reaction involving the gain of oxygen or the loss of hydrogen

     **ii)** A reaction involving the loss of oxygen or the gain of hydrogen

**g) 10 letters**   Pieces of metal or carbon which allow electric current to enter and leave during electrolysis

**h) 11 letters**   **i)** The state in which a chemical reaction proceeds at the same rate as its reverse reaction

     **ii)** The sum of the atomic masses of all atoms in a molecule (2 words)

**i) 12 letters**   **i)** Elements in Group 1 of the periodic table (2 words)

     **ii)** The number of an element's place in the periodic table; the number of protons an element has in the nucleus of its atom (2 words)

     **iii)** The process by which an electric current flowing through a liquid containing ions causes the liquid to undergo chemical decomposition

     **iv)** The process of two or more atoms losing or gaining electrons to become charged ions (2 words)

**j) 13 letters**   **i)** Materials with a very small grain size

     **ii)** The removal of a solid from a solution

**k) 14 letters**   **i)** Reaction between an acid and a base which forms a neutral solution

     **ii)** Materials that have one or more properties that can be altered (2 words)

**l) 15 letters**   A bond between two atoms in which both atoms share one electron (2 words)

**m) 18 letters**   **i)** A reaction which gives off heat (2 words)

     **ii)** A reaction in which products react to reform the original reactants (2 words)

**n) 19 letters**   A reaction which takes in heat from the surroundings (2 words)

# Physics Unit 2

## Speed

**1** What is the definition of speed?

.................................................................................................................................

**2** What two things do you need to know to work out the speed of an object?

**a)** ......................................................................................................................

**b)** ......................................................................................................................

**3** A cyclist travels 60km in 2 hours. What is his average speed in kilometres per hour?

.................................................................................................................................

## Distance–Time Graphs

**4** The distance-time graph opposite shows a cyclist's journey.

**a)** Describe the motion of the cyclist from…

    **i)** O to A..................................................................................

    **ii)** A to B.................................................................................

    **iii)** B to C...............................................................................

**b)** What was the total distance travelled by the cyclist?

.................................................................................................................................

**c)** How long did the journey take?

.................................................................................................................................

**d)** Calculate the average speed of the cyclist for the first 30 minutes of the journey.

.................................................................................................................................

## Velocity

**5** Tick the correct answer. Velocity is…

**a)** another way of saying speed ☐

**b)** how fast an object is accelerating ☐

**c)** a way to describe the direction an object is facing ☐

**d)** the speed and direction of travel of an object ☐

**e)** a way to describe the type of motion of an object. ☐

## Acceleration

**1** **a)** What is the definition of acceleration?

....................................................................................................................................................................

**b)** What two things do you need to know to work out acceleration?

**i)** ...........................................................................................................................................................

**ii)** ..........................................................................................................................................................

**2** How is acceleration measured? Tick the correct answer.

**a)** metres per second (m/s) ☐     **c)** miles per hour (mph) ☐

**b)** metres per second$^2$ (m/s$^2$) ☐     **d)** kilometres per hour (km/h) ☐

**3** **a)** A car accelerates uniformly from rest to a speed of 15m/s in a time of 5s. Calculate the acceleration of the car.

....................................................................................................................................................................

**b)** A train accelerates from a speed of 20m/s to 34m/s in 4s. Calculate the acceleration of the train.

....................................................................................................................................................................

**c)** A fighter plane travelling at a velocity of 40m/s lands on an aircraft carrier, where it is stopped in a time of 2s. Calculate the deceleration of the plane.

....................................................................................................................................................................

## Velocity-Time Graphs

**4** The graph alongside shows a car travelling along a road.

**a)** What is the car doing for the first second?

....................................................................................................

**b)** What is the car doing for the next four seconds?

....................................................................................................

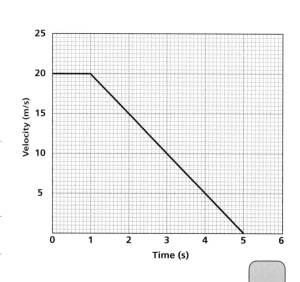

# How Science Works

**To answer the questions on this page, you will have to recall scientific facts and draw upon your knowledge of how science works, e.g. scientific procedures, issues and ideas.**

1 An Alsatian dog, Rex, was chasing a ball in the park. His owner threw the ball 20m away and Rex ran after it for 30 seconds at a constant speed. He reached the ball and stopped for 5 seconds whilst he picked it up, before running back to his owner also at a constant speed. In the meantime however, his owner had moved 5m closer to Rex, so the dog only had to run 15m which took him 25 seconds. He dropped the ball at his owner's feet and was then stationary for a further 10 seconds before his owner threw the ball again.

Construct a distance-time graph for Rex's movements on the axes below.

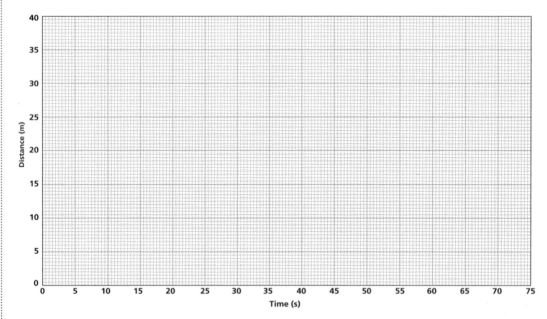

2 The table below shows the velocity and time of a motorcyclist for the first 20 seconds of her journey.

| Velocity (m/s) | 0 | 5 | 10 | 10 | 10 | 12 | 14 | 14 | 15 | 16 | 16 |
|---|---|---|---|---|---|---|---|---|---|---|---|
| Time (s) | 0 | 2 | 4 | 6 | 8 | 10 | 12 | 14 | 16 | 18 | 20 |

Construct a velocity–time graph of the motorcyclist's journey on the axes below.

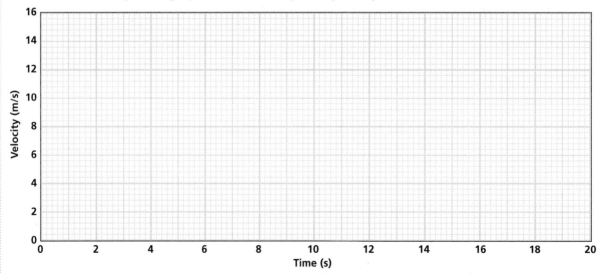

**To answer the questions on this page, you will have to recall scientific facts and draw upon your knowledge of how science works, e.g. scientific procedures, issues and ideas.**

**1** The distance–time graph on the right shows Paula doing her shopping.

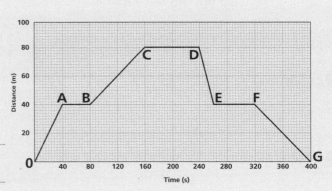

**a)** In terms of movement, describe the first four minutes of Paula's shopping trip.

_____

_____

**b)** In which region – BC, CD, DE, EF, or FG – was she travelling the fastest? _____

**c)** Calculate Paula's speed in the following regions.

   **i)** OA: _____    **ii)** BC: _____    **iii)** DE: _____

**2** The velocity–time graph below shows a train moving from one station to another.

**a)** Describe the motion of the train for the first four minutes.

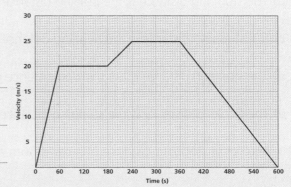

_____

_____

_____

**b)** Calculate the two accelerations of the train.

_____

_____

**c)** Calculate the deceleration of the train.

_____

**d)** Calculate the total distance travelled by the train.

_____

_____

# Physics Unit 2

## Forces

**1** Complete this sentence: A stationary object exerts a downward force on the surface it rests upon. The surface exerts an upward force that is...

**2** Explain what a resultant force is.

**3** What is friction?

## Stopping Distances

**4** Tick the correct statement.

**a)** The braking distance is the stopping distance plus the thinking distance. ☐

**b)** The stopping distance is the braking distance plus the time it takes the car to stop. ☐

**c)** The stopping distance is the thinking distance plus the braking distance. ☐

**d)** The stopping distance is the thinking distance plus the time it takes the driver to realise he needs to stop. ☐

**e)** The thinking distance is the stopping distance plus the braking distance. ☐

**5** If the overall stopping distance of a car is 56m and the thinking distance is 16m, what is the braking distance?

**6** What effect does an increase in the thinking distance have on...

**a)** the braking distance?

**b)** the overall stopping distance?

**7** List three factors that can affect the stopping distance of a car.

**a)**

**b)**

**c)**

## How Forces Affect Movement

**1** Tick the correct option to complete the sentence. If the forces acting on an object are not equal and opposite, the force is...

**a)** balanced ☐

**b)** unbalanced ☐

**c)** resultant ☐

**d)** centripetal ☐

**2** What happens to a stationary object if an unbalanced force acts on it?

**3** What happens to a moving object travelling at a constant speed if a balanced force acts on it?

**4** What happens to a moving object travelling at a constant speed if an unbalanced force acts on it?

**5** Nick is trying to push his car down the road, but he finds that by himself he is unable to get the car to move. He calls his dad over to help and together they push the car which starts to move and then accelerates.

**a)** Explain what would happen to the speed of the car if **i)** Nick and then **ii)** Nick and his dad stop pushing.

**i)**

**ii)**

**b)** Name the force that initially stops Nick from being able to push the car.

# Physics Unit 2

## Force, Mass and Acceleration

**1** What two things does the acceleration of an object depend on?

**a)** ................................................................. **b)** .................................................................

**2** For each of the following questions, explain your answer.

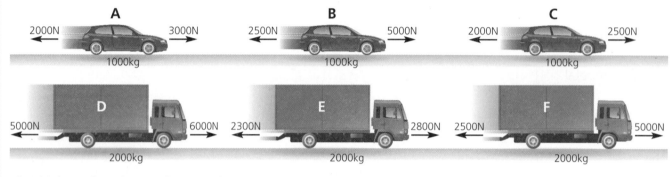

**a)** Which car has the smallest acceleration? ..........................................................................

**b)** Which car has the greatest acceleration? ..........................................................................

**c)** Which lorry has the smallest acceleration? .......................................................................

**d)** Which lorry has the greatest acceleration? .......................................................................

**e)** Will car B or lorry F have the greatest acceleration? .......................................................

**f)** Which two vehicles have the same acceleration? .............................................................

**3** Write down the formula showing the relationship between mass, force and acceleration.

................................................................................................................................................

**4** A car is moving at a constant speed of 30m/s. The combined mass of the car and the driver is 1000kg.

**a)** If the driving force is 3000N, what is the value of the frictional force?

................................................................................................................................................

**b)** If the driver increases the driving force to 4000N, calculate the acceleration of the car.

................................................................................................................................................

**5** A motorcycle is moving along a straight road. The total mass of the motorcyclist and the bike is 250kg. The motorcyclist accelerates at 2m/s$^2$. Calculate the force needed to produce this acceleration.

................................................................................................................................................

## Terminal Velocity

**1 a)** Anil jumps out of a plane. He does not initially open his parachute, but freefalls towards the ground. As he is falling, he accelerates. Explain, in terms of the forces acting on Anil, why he accelerates.

_____

_____

_____

**b)** What happens to the air resistance as he falls?

_____

_____

**c)** Anil will eventually stop accelerating, and will start to fall at a steady speed. Explain why this is so, and what this steady speed is called.

_____

_____

_____

**d)** After 40 seconds of freefall, Anil opens his parachute. What effect will this have on the air resistance acting upon him?

_____

**e)** What happens to his speed now?

_____

**f)** Eventually Anil will stop decelerating. Explain why.

_____

_____

**g)** Anil has reached terminal velocity twice in his jump. Will his terminal velocity be the same at both points? Explain your answer.

_____

_____

_____

# How Science Works

**To answer the questions on this page, you will have to recall scientific facts and draw upon your knowledge of how science works, e.g. scientific procedures, issues and ideas.**

**1** As part of a training exercise, a fighter plane pilot is required to take his plane into a steep dive, only levelling off when he reaches a certain height. The table below shows the velocity of the plane at 4 second intervals, from when the pilot first goes into the dive up until the point where he has reached the required height and pulls out of the dive.

| Velocity (km/s) | 150 | 210 | 260 | 290 | 330 | 360 | 360 | 360 |
|---|---|---|---|---|---|---|---|---|
| Time (s) | 4 | 8 | 12 | 16 | 20 | 24 | 28 | 32 |

**a)** Plot the plane's dive on the graph below.

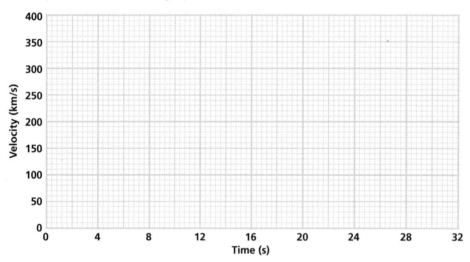

**b)** Why is the slope steeper at first?

......................................................................................................................................

......................................................................................................................................

**c)** What does the flat horizontal line indicate?

......................................................................................................................................

**2** **a)** Write down the formula for calculating weight.

......................................................................................................................................

**b)** A number of masses are shown below. Calculate their weight on Earth, if the gravitational force strength is 10N/kg.

**i)** Mass of 2kg...............................................................................................................

**ii)** Mass of 250g.............................................................................................................

**iii)** Mass of 10kg.............................................................................................................

**iv)** Mass of 75g...............................................................................................................

## Work

**1** What is the relationship between work done, force and distance?

.................................................................................................................................

.................................................................................................................................

**2** Tony lifts a parcel of weight 100N onto a shelf that is 2m above the ground. Calculate the work done in lifting the parcel onto the shelf.

.................................................................................................................................

.................................................................................................................................

**3** Describe what elastic potential energy is.

.................................................................................................................................

.................................................................................................................................

## Kinetic Energy

**4** What is kinetic energy?

.................................................................................................................................

.................................................................................................................................

**5** What two things does kinetic energy depend on?

.................................................................................................................................

.................................................................................................................................

**6** A truck of mass 2000kg and a car of mass 1000kg are travelling down a motorway at the same speed. Which one has the greatest kinetic energy? Explain why.

.................................................................................................................................

.................................................................................................................................

**7** Two cars of the same mass are travelling down a road. Explain how one car could have more kinetic energy than the other.

.................................................................................................................................

.................................................................................................................................

**8** A car of mass 1000kg moves along a road at a constant speed of 20m/s. Calculate its kinetic energy.

.................................................................................................................................

.................................................................................................................................

**9** A truck of mass 32 000kg moves along a road with a speed of 10m/s. Calculate its kinetic energy.

.................................................................................................................................

.................................................................................................................................

# How Science Works

**To answer the questions on this page, you will have to recall scientific facts and draw upon your knowledge of how science works, e.g. scientific procedures, issues and ideas.**

**1** Name three different forms of energy that kinetic energy could be transformed into.

**a)** ............................................................................................................................................

**b)** ............................................................................................................................................

**c)** ............................................................................................................................................

**2** In the following examples, describe the form(s) of energy that kinetic energy is being transformed into.

**a)** A moving turbine in a power station. .................................................................................

**b)** A falling squash ball hitting the ground. ............................................................................

**c)** A tennis ball bouncing from the floor into the air. ............................................................

**d)** A car braking. ....................................................................................................................

**e)** A person bouncing on a trampoline. .................................................................................

**3** A bungee jumper, jumping off a bridge has kinetic energy. Describe how this energy is transformed when he reaches the end of the bungee cord.

....................................................................................................................................................

....................................................................................................................................................

....................................................................................................................................................

**4** Can you think of another example of the transformation of kinetic energy to another form of energy? Explain how the energy would transform, the benefits of the energy transformation, and any problems created. Use the Internet, library, or another secondary source to help you.

....................................................................................................................................................

....................................................................................................................................................

....................................................................................................................................................

....................................................................................................................................................

....................................................................................................................................................

....................................................................................................................................................

## Momentum

**1** Does a stationary car have momentum? Explain your answer.

......................................................................................................................................

......................................................................................................................................

**2** What two things does momentum depend on?

**a)** ...............................................................................................................................

**b)** ...............................................................................................................................

**3 a)** Write down the equation for calculating momentum.

......................................................................................................................................

**b)** Calculate the momentum of a jogger of mass 80kg running at a velocity of 0.4m/s.

......................................................................................................................................

**c)** Calculate the momentum of a car of mass 900kg travelling at a velocity of 20m/s.

......................................................................................................................................

**d)** A truck is moving with a velocity of 18m/s. Calculate its mass if it has a momentum of 61 000m/s.

......................................................................................................................................

......................................................................................................................................

## Magnitude and Direction

**4 a)** A car of mass 1200kg is travelling at a velocity of 15m/s. What happens to its velocity and its momentum if the car then travels in the opposite direction with a speed of 15m/s?

......................................................................................................................................

......................................................................................................................................

**b)** Calculate the momentum of the car when it travels in the opposite direction.

......................................................................................................................................

......................................................................................................................................

# Physics Unit 2

## Force and Change in Momentum

**1** In terms of momentum, what happens when an unbalanced force acts on a stationary object?

.......................................................................................................................................................

.......................................................................................................................................................

**2** What two things can happen to momentum when an unbalanced force acts on a moving object?

**a)** .............................................................................................................................................

**b)** .............................................................................................................................................

**3** The extent of change in momentum depends on two factors. What are they?

**a)** .............................................................................................................................................

**b)** .............................................................................................................................................

**4** How can change in momentum be calculated?

.......................................................................................................................................................

**5** Jenny is playing squash. The ball is coming towards her at a momentum of 5kg m/s. She swings with a force that acts on the ball for 0.9 seconds and the ball then speeds off towards the front wall with a momentum of 10kg m/s.

**a)** What is the change in momentum of the ball?

.......................................................................................................................................................

.......................................................................................................................................................

**b)** With what force did Jenny's racket hit the ball?

.......................................................................................................................................................

.......................................................................................................................................................

**c)** How could Jenny increase the momentum and velocity of the ball, without increasing the force applied?

.......................................................................................................................................................

.......................................................................................................................................................

## Collisions and Explosions

**1** In a collision or explosion, momentum is conserved. What does this mean?

_____

_____

_____

**2** Two cars are travelling in the same direction along a road. Car A collides with car B and they lock together. Calculate their velocity after the collision.

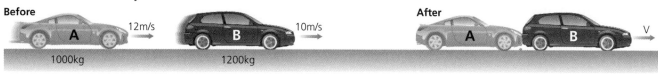

_____

_____

_____

_____

**3** Two cars are travelling towards each other along a road. Car A collides with car B and they stick together. Calculate their velocity after the collision.

_____

_____

_____

**4** A gun is fired as below. If the recoil velocity of the gun is 2m/s, calculate the velocity of the bullet.

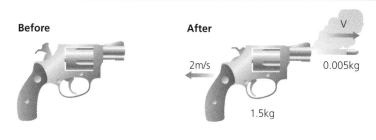

_____

_____

_____

_____

# How Science Works

**To answer the questions on this page, you will have to recall scientific facts and draw upon your knowledge of how science works, e.g. scientific procedures, issues and ideas.**

**1 a)** In terms of momentum, what happens to a passenger in the front of a car if the car crashes and comes to a sudden halt and they are not wearing a seat belt?

_____

_____

**b)** In terms of momentum, how does a seat belt work?

_____

_____

_____

**2** In terms of momentum, explain how a crumple zone in a car works.

_____

_____

_____

**3** Name one other safety feature in a car that is concerned with momentum and explain how it works.

_____

_____

_____

_____

_____

_____

_____

_____

_____

## Static Electricity

**1** **a)** The picture opposite shows Rachel charging a balloon with static electricity. Explain how the balloon gains a positive charge.

_____

_____

**b)** What charge will Rachel's jumper have?

_____

**2** Thomas was in a classroom at school where there was a nylon carpet on the floor. He found that if he walked across the classroom and touched a metal radiator he got an electric shock. Explain why.

_____

_____

## Repulsion and Attraction

**3** An ebonite rod is moved near to a second ebonite rod, which is suspended on a string. What will happen to the suspended rod? Explain your answer.

_____

**4** An ebonite rod is moved near to a suspended perspex rod. What will happen to the suspended rod? Explain your answer.

_____

## Uses of Static

**5** Give two examples of how static electricity can be used in everyday life.

**a)** _____ **b)** _____

**6** Explain how a smoke precipitator works using electrostatic charges.

_____

_____

_____

_____

# Physics Unit 2

## Uses of Static (continued)

**1** The following mixed-up statements describe how a photocopier works.

**a)**
> ... charged impression of the plate attracts tiny specs of black powder...

**b)**
> ... paper is heated to fix the final image...

**c)**
> ... copying plate is electrically charged...

**d)**
> ... powder is transferred from the plate to the paper...

**e)**
> ... image of the page to be copied is projected onto the plate...

**f)**
> ... charge leaks away due to light, leaving an electrostatic impression of page...

What is the correct order in which they should appear? ☐ ☐ ☐ ☐ ☐ ☐

## Discharge of Static Electricity

**2** Static electricity can be discharged. Explain what this means.

....................................................................................................................

....................................................................................................................

**3** Why are metals good conductors of electricity?

....................................................................................................................

....................................................................................................................

**4** Explain how a conductor, attached to a positively charged dome, discharges electricity.

....................................................................................................................

....................................................................................................................

**HT**

**5** What causes electricity to flow though the air?

....................................................................................................................

....................................................................................................................

**6** How is the energy flow in a conductor attached to a negatively charged dome different to one attached to a positively charged dome?

....................................................................................................................

....................................................................................................................

**To answer the questions on this page, you will have to recall scientific facts and draw upon your knowledge of how science works, e.g. scientific procedures, issues and ideas.**

**1** Why is it important to ensure that static electricity is discharged safely?

........................................................................................................................

........................................................................................................................

**2** During the refuelling of planes, care needs to be taken to avoid dangerous electrical discharges.

**a)** Why could there be a discharge?

........................................................................

........................................................................

**b)** Explain how this discharge can be made safe.

Fuel pipe

........................................................................................................................

........................................................................................................................

**3 a)** Explain why static electricity is a real hazard at a petrol station.

........................................................................................................................

........................................................................................................................

**b)** Give two precautions that should be taken at a petrol station to avoid the discharge of static electricity.

**i)** ................................................................................................................

**ii)** ...............................................................................................................

**4 a)** Explain how computers can be damaged by static electricity.

........................................................................................................................

........................................................................................................................

**b)** What precaution can computer technicians take to avoid damaging computers with static electricity? Explain your answer.

........................................................................................................................

........................................................................................................................

# How Science Works

**(continued)**

**5** What is lightning?

_____

_____

_____

**6** Explain how a lightning conductor protects a building from lighting.

_____

_____

_____

_____

**7** During a thunderstorm, explain why it can be dangerous to…

**a)** stand under a tree

_____

**b)** hold an umbrella with a metal tip

_____

_____

**c)** stand in the middle of a field.

_____

_____

**8** Some people attach a strip of rubber to their car, which extends to the ground, to help avoid electric shocks. In theory, how could this help?

_____

_____

_____

_____

## Circuits

**1** Below are five simple circuits (all the cells and lamps are identical).

| A | B | C | D | E |

a) Which circuit has the greatest potential difference? ........................................................................

b) Which circuit has the least potential difference? ........................................................................

c) Which circuit has the greatest resistance? ........................................................................

d) Which circuit has the least resistance? ........................................................................

**2** Which circuit would have the brightest lamp(s)? Explain why.

........................................................................................................................................................

........................................................................................................................................................

........................................................................................................................................................

**3** Which circuit would have the dimmest lamp(s)? Explain why.

........................................................................................................................................................

........................................................................................................................................................

........................................................................................................................................................

**4** Which two circuits have the same current flowing through them? Explain why.

........................................................................................................................................................

........................................................................................................................................................

## Potential Difference and Current

**5** What is potential difference measured in?

........................................................................................................................................................

**6** What is current measured in?

........................................................................................................................................................

# Physics Unit 2

## Resistance

**1** How would you define resistance in a circuit?

........................................................................................................................................................

**2** How are potential difference, current and resistance related?

........................................................................................................................................................

**3** For the circuits shown below, each cell provides a potential difference of 1.5V. For each circuit calculate
**i)** the potential difference supplied, **ii)** total resistance, **iii)** ammeter reading, and **iv)** $V_1$ and $V_2$

a)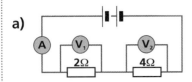

b)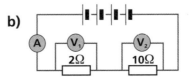

c)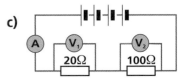

**i)** ..............................................    **i)** ..............................................    **i)** ..............................................

**ii)** ..............................................    **ii)** ..............................................    **ii)** ..............................................

**iii)** ..............................................    **iii)** ..............................................    **iii)** ..............................................

**iv)** ..............................................    **iv)** ..............................................    **iv)** ..............................................

## Resistance of Components

**4** Below are three current-potential difference graphs. Which graph corresponds to the following components?

A 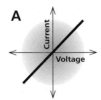    B 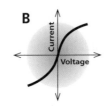    C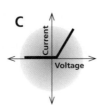

**a)** A diode. ................................................................................................................................

**b)** A resistor at a constant temperature. ...................................................................................

**c)** A filament lamp. ..................................................................................................................

**5** Name the component...

**a)** whose resistance decreases as the light intensity on it increases ..................................................

**b)** which allows a current to flow through it in one direction only ..................................................

**c)** whose resistance decreases as its temperature increases. ..................................................

## Series and Parallel Circuits

**1** For each circuit shown below, write the missing values for current and potential difference in the spaces provided (the lamps in each circuit are identical).

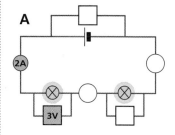

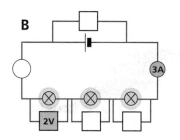

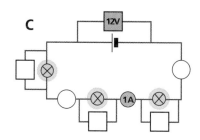

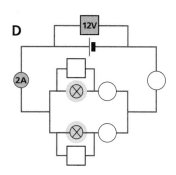

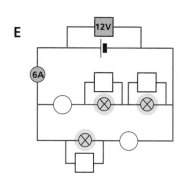

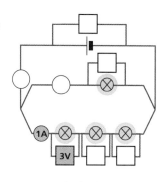

**2** In the series circuit shown opposite each cell provides a p.d. of 1.5V.

**a)** What is the total resistance of the circuit?...............................................

**b)** What is the p.d. across the 10 Ω resistor?.................................................

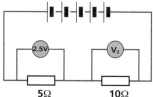

**3** For the parallel circuit shown opposite, answer the following:

**a)** What is the total resistance of branch X of the circuit?......................

**b)** What is the total resistance of branch Y of the circuit?......................

**c)** What is the current through…

**i)** branch X?................................................

**ii)** branch Y? .............................................

**d)** The potential difference of the supply is 10V.

**i)** What is the value of the p.d, $V_1$?.................................................

**ii)** What is the value of the p.d, $V_2$?.................................................

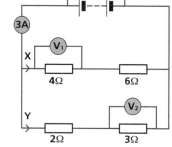

# How Science Works

**To answer the questions on this page, you will have to recall scientific facts and draw upon your knowledge of how science works, e.g. scientific procedures, issues and ideas.**

**1** For each of the following electrical symbols write down the name of the component they represent.

a)    b)    c)    d)

.................................  .................................  .................................  .................................

**2** Draw the symbols for these electrical components.

**a)** Battery.................................  **b)** Variable Resistor.................................  **c)** Thermistor.................................  **d)** Switch (closed).................................

**3** In the space provided, draw a circuit diagram to represent the circuit (below). Include on your diagram:

**a)** an open switch; **b)** an ammeter to measure the current; **c)** a voltmeter to measure the p.d across the cells.

## Applying Circuit Diagrams to Practical Solutions

**4** Name one example of a simple circuit being used in an everyday situation. Explain how the circuit is used and draw a circuit diagram to explain your answer.

.................................................................................................

.................................................................................................

.................................................................................................

.................................................................................................

.................................................................................................

.................................................................................................

.................................................................................................

.................................................................................................

.................................................................................................

.................................................................................................

## Currents

**1** How does an alternating current differ from a direct current?

........................................................................................................................................

........................................................................................................................................

**2** What is the voltage of UK mains electricity? Tick the correct answer.

**a)** 235V ☐ **c)** 230V ☐

**b)** 240V ☐ **d)** 245V ☐

## The Three-Pin Plug

**3** Name three everyday electrical appliances that are connected to the mains electricity supply.

**a)** ........................................ **b)** ........................................ **c)** ........................................

**4 a)** Complete the diagram of the 3-pin plug by adding any wires, cables and connections. Label all the parts, including which colours the different wires should be.

**b)** What is the casing made of, and why?

........................................................................................................................................

**c)** What are the inner cores of the wires made of, and why?

........................................................................................................................................

**d)** What are the pins in the plug made of, and why?

........................................................................................................................................

**HT**

**5 a)** What kind of voltages does the live wire vary between?

........................................................................................................................................

**b)** What voltage is the neutral wire always close to?

........................................................................................................................................

## Circuit Breakers and Fuses

**1 a)** What is the purpose of a circuit breaker or a fuse?

........................................................................................................................................

**b)** Explain how a circuit breaker works.

........................................................................................................................................

........................................................................................................................................

........................................................................................................................................

**c)** Explain how a fuse works.

........................................................................................................................................

........................................................................................................................................

........................................................................................................................................

**d)** Are there any advantages to using a circuit breaker rather than a fuse?

........................................................................................................................................

........................................................................................................................................

## Earthing

**2** In a metal toaster, the earth wire is connected to the outer casing of the toaster.

**a)** If the brown live wire became loose and touched the outer casing of the toaster, how would the earth wire make the appliance safe?

........................................................................................................................................

........................................................................................................................................

........................................................................................................................................

**b)** What two things together protect the toaster and the user?

........................................................................................................................................

........................................................................................................................................

# How Science Works

**To answer the questions on this page, you will have to recall scientific facts and draw upon your knowledge of how science works, e.g. scientific procedures, issues and ideas.**

**1** For the 3-pin plug shown opposite, write down four faults.

a) ................................................................

b) ................................................................

c) ................................................................

d) ................................................................

Nail

Blue wire

Yellow and green wire wire

Brown wire

**2** Explain what you would do to fix the following faults on a 3-pin plug.

**a)** A bare wire showing.

................................................................................................................

**b)** A piece of silver foil being used for a fuse.

................................................................................................................

**c)** A loose cable grip.

................................................................................................................

**d)** A frayed cable.

................................................................................................................

**3** Explain why you should never touch a socket with wet hands.

................................................................................................................

................................................................................................................

................................................................................................................

**4** Why should you never overload a plug socket?

................................................................................................................

................................................................................................................

# How Science Works

To answer the questions on this page, you will have to recall scientific facts and draw upon your knowledge of how science works, e.g. scientific procedures, issues and ideas.

**1** Three traces from an oscilloscope screen are shown below.

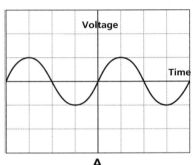

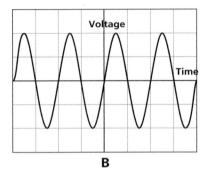

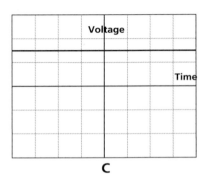

**A**       **B**       **C**

**a)** Which of the three traces shows a direct current?

_____

**HT**

**b)** If the peak voltage on trace A is 5V, what is the peak voltage of trace B?

_____

**c)** If the frequency of trace B is 50Hz, what is the frequency of trace A?

_____

**2** Look at trace A in Question 1. On the screen below sketch a trace of an alternating current which is half the frequency, and three times the voltage, of trace A.

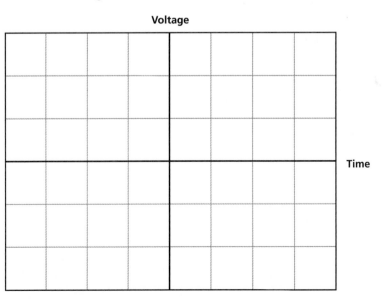

## Power

**1 a)** What is an electric current?

............................................................................................................................

**b)** What unit is used to measure electric current?

............................................................................................................................

**2** Write down the equation by which power, potential difference and current are related.

............................................................................................................................

**3** An electric motor works at a current of 3A and a potential difference of 24V. What is the power of the motor?

............................................................................................................................

**4** A 4W light bulb works at a current of 2A. What is the potential difference?

............................................................................................................................

## Charge and Energy Transformation

**5** How is charge calculated?

............................................................................................................................

**6** How is energy transformation calculated?

............................................................................................................................

**7** In the circuit opposite, the lamp is switched on for 5 minutes and the reading on the ammeter is 3A. Calculate...

6V

**a)** the charge that flows...............................................................................................

**b)** the energy transformed...........................................................................................

**c)** the power of the lamp in the circuit.......................................................................

# How Science Works

To answer the questions on this page, you will have to recall scientific facts and draw upon your knowledge of how science works, e.g. scientific procedures, issues and ideas.

**1 a)** Why do fuses come in different sizes?

**b)** What would happen if you used a 3A fuse for a device that was running on a 13V current?

**c)** What would happen if you used a 13A fuse for a device that was running on a 2V current?

**2** What is the formula for working out the current of an appliance?

**3** It is important that electrical appliances are fitted with the correct size of fuse. In the table below, work out the normal working current for each appliance and state the correct fuse needed for each appliance.

| Appliance | Power rating (W) | P.D. (V) | Working current | Fuse size (1A, 3A, 5A, 13A) |
|---|---|---|---|---|
| Iron | 920 | 230 | | |
| Kettle | 2300 | 230 | | |
| Hi-Fi | 80 | 240 | | |
| Vacuum | 1400 | 230 | | |
| Toaster | 720 | 240 | | |

**4** You buy a brand new microwave with a power rating of 850W and potential difference of 230V. Calculate the size of the fuse required for the appliance.

## Atoms

**1** Why does an atom have no overall charge?

**2** *An electron has a negative mass.* Is this statement **true** or **false**?

**3** If you know the number of protons in an atom, is it possible to deduce how many electrons there are? Explain your answer.

**4** Tick the statement that provides best definition for an isotope.

**a)** Atoms of the same element with a different number of protons ☐

**b)** Atoms of the same element with a different number of neutrons ☐

**c)** Atoms of a different element with the same number of neutrons ☐

**d)** The number of protons in an element ☐

**5** What is the mass number of an element?

## Ionisation

**6 a)** What is an ion?

**b)** How can radioactive particles create ions?

**7** Name two types of ionising radiation.

**a)**

**b)**

# Physics Unit 2

## Radioactive Decay and Background Radiation

**8** What is radioactive decay?

........................................................................................

........................................................................................

**9** Explain how beta radiation is formed.

........................................................................................

........................................................................................

........................................................................................

**10** Why is gamma radiation different from alpha and beta radiation?

........................................................................................

........................................................................................

**11** Explain why there is radiation all around us, and give two examples of where this kind of radiation comes from.

........................................................................................

........................................................................................

**12** Draw an accurate pie chart in the space below to show the proportions of radiation from man-made sources compared to that from natural sources.

**HT**

**To answer the questions on this page, you will have to recall scientific facts and draw upon your knowledge of how science works, e.g. scientific procedures, issues and ideas.**

**1 a)** Who came up with the 'plum pudding' model of the atom, and what theory did he propose?

..................................................................................................................................................

..................................................................................................................................................

**b)** Sketch a labelled diagram of the plum pudding model.

**2 a)** What experiment did Ernest Rutherford design in 1911? ...........................................................

**b)** Describe, in as much detail as possible, what Rutherford did in his experiment.

..................................................................................................................................................

..................................................................................................................................................

..................................................................................................................................................

**c)** Explain what happened to the alpha particles in the experiment.

..................................................................................................................................................

..................................................................................................................................................

**d)** Explain why some of the particles were deflected back towards the source.

..................................................................................................................................................

..................................................................................................................................................

**e)** What conclusions on the structure of the atom did Rutherford draw from his experiment?

..................................................................................................................................................

..................................................................................................................................................

## Nuclear Fusion and Fission

**1** Explain the difference between nuclear fission and nuclear fusion.

................................................................................................................................

................................................................................................................................

**2 a)** What happens during nuclear fusion?

................................................................................................................................

................................................................................................................................

**b)** What is produced during nuclear fusion?

................................................................................................................................

**3** Why is nuclear fusion a self-sustaining reaction?

................................................................................................................................

**4** Explain how the Sun produces light and heat energy.

................................................................................................................................

................................................................................................................................

**5** Name two substances commonly used in nuclear fission.

**a)** ................................................................................................................................

**b)** ................................................................................................................................

**6** Nuclear fission can be used on a large scale in a nuclear reactor. Once fission has started it continues by itself. Explain why.

................................................................................................................................

................................................................................................................................

................................................................................................................................

................................................................................................................................

## Nuclear Fusion and Fission (continued)

**7** The diagram below shows small-scale nuclear fission. Write the following labels in the correct places on the diagram.

**Energy**     **New radioactive nuclei are formed**     **Uranium nucleus**

**Further neutrons**     **Neutron**     **Unstable nucleus, fissions occurs and nucleus splits**

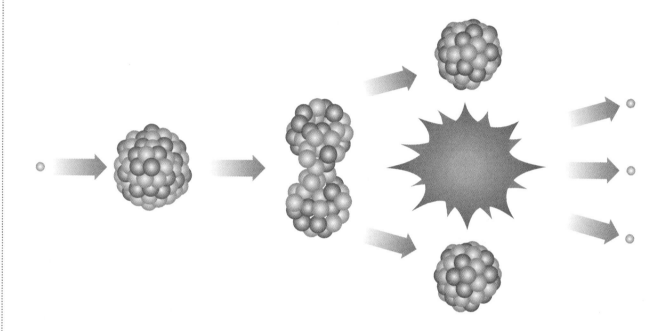

**8 a)** What are the products of nuclear fission?

**i)** ................................................................................................................................................

**ii)** ...............................................................................................................................................

**b)** Are these products **radioactive** or **non-radioactive**?

....................................................................................................................................................

**c)** What potential problem does this pose?

....................................................................................................................................................

....................................................................................................................................................

# Physics Unit 2

**1** Fill in the crossword below using the following clues:

## Across

**1)** A constant falling speed (8,8)

**6)** How fast an object is travelling (5)

**8)** Can be either direct or alternating (7)

**10)** Atoms of the same element with different numbers of neutrons (7)

**11)** The type of electricity you would create if you rubbed your hair with a balloon (6)

**12)** The amount of matter in a body (4)

**14)** What happens when two like charges come together? (9)

**16)** A neutrally charged subatomic particle (7)

**17)** Allows current to flow in one direction only (5)

## Down

**1)** A resistor that is affected by changes in temperature (10)

**2)** A state of motion (8)

**3)** Measured in joules (6)

**4)** A device which trips a circuit (7-7)

**5)** A measure of force (6)

**7)** A resistive force (8)

**9)** A negatively charged subatomic particle (8)

**13)** A positively charged subatomic particle (6)

**15)** Charged particles (4)